Music Therapy Improvisation for Groups:

Essential Leadership Competencies

Susan C. Gardstrom

Barcelona PUBLISHERS

Music Therapy Improvisation for Groups:
Essential Leadership Competencies
By Susan C. Gardstrom

Copyright © 2007by Barcelona Publishers

Print ISBN 13: 9781891278495

E-ISBN: 9781891278709

Distributed throughout the world by:
Barcelona Publishers
2427 Bond St.
University Park, IL 60484
In USA, toll free: 866-620-6943
www.barcelonapublishers.com
SAN 298-6299

Cover design:
© 2007 Frank McShane

ACKNOWLEDGMENTS

I wish to express my gratitude to a few individuals who assisted me during the production of this book and without whom I would not have been able to complete it.

First, I offer my appreciation to Dr. Kenneth E. Bruscia for encouraging me to write, for always finding time to answer my questions (and pose his own), and for providing the scholarly reservoir from which so many of the notions herein—and scores of other resources in the field of music therapy—are drawn.

I also thank Jim Hiller, my collaborator at the University of Dayton, for teaching me a lot of what I know about clinical music improvisation and instilling in me a passion for and profound belief in the method.

Finally, I thank my son, Dillon, for his patient support, and my sister, Karen Gardstrom, for her eager and thorough editorial help with this and many other scholarly endeavors.

Table of Contents

Chapter One

INTRODUCTION

THE EVOLUTION OF THIS BOOK

I have been teaching an introductory course in clinical improvisation to undergraduate music therapy and music education students since 1999 and conducting workshops on the method since 2000. In short, when I began teaching at my university, I inherited an improvisation course that had been proposed by a predecessor but had never been taught. I had not been trained in how to instruct improvisation, so I knew that I would have to rely heavily on published resources and help from other professionals to develop the specifics of the course. Much to my surprise and dismay, I found only two books available on the subject of clinical improvisation at that time, *Improvisational Models of Music Therapy* (Bruscia, 1987) and *Healing Heritage* (Robbins & Robbins, 1998). *Improvisational Models* is a one-of-a-kind, comprehensive reference that systematically and thoroughly describes salient features of over 25 models of clinical improvisation and their accompanying techniques, dynamics, and processes. It seemed to me that Bruscia's book could provide important theoretical foundations for instruction. One chapter in particular, "Sixty-Four Clinical Techniques" (pp. 533–557) supplied helpful clues about specific skills that would be necessary for the facilitation of improvisation. This was a good start; however, Bruscia's book was not designed to serve as a formula for specific skill development in undergraduate training and thus could not serve as a primary text for this introductory course.

I thought that *Healing Heritage* also could be a valuable resource for the music therapist in training, in that it chronicles important historical information about the life and work of pioneers in the field and emphasizes the importance of various musical elements and their unique power in the therapeutic process. Yet, as I reviewed this publication, it became obvious that its value was also as a supplemental rather than primary text. There were two reasons for this. First, the book clearly represents one specific paradigm, *Nordoff & Robbins Music Therapy* (sometimes referred to as *Creative Music Therapy*). This approach, perhaps the most thoroughly archived of all models of clinical improvisation, originally called for therapists to work in teams of two, with one person improvising at the piano and the other individual assisting the child in his or her responses to the music and the clinical intentions of the pianist (Bruscia, 1987; Robbins & Robbins, 1991). The material in *Healing Heritage* reflects the primacy of piano in this approach; the material revolves around tonal (melodic and harmonic) aspects of music-making. Only in passing do the authors of *Healing Heritage* make mention of rhythmic features or textual/lyrical aspects of improvisation, both of which I believed were essential for students to incorporate into their practice. Second, the training from which the transcriptions originated was not designed for undergraduates, but rather for 15 students who already possessed a degree or diploma in music and who had demonstrated some level of musical competence. (Most were pianists, and four had worked as therapists for up to five years.) Essential aspects of the sequential development of clinical improvisation skills are missing from this book.

Looking for some guidance, I called friends and colleagues in my region who were teaching at the undergraduate level. I found that, with one exception, the individuals I contacted did not teach self-contained undergraduate courses in improvisation, mostly because they did not feel equipped to do so, having received little or no training themselves. (A recent survey by Hiller [2006] has substantiated that board-certified music therapists report a lack of training in the use of clinical music improvisation during undergraduate courses and internships.) In most cases, my colleagues either "touched on" improvisation in the context of other skill-based units or courses or relied on instructors within their departments to initiate students in music improvisation concepts and applications, often with an orientation toward jazz or Orff-Schulwerk. No one with whom I spoke taught a course specifically in group improvisation, which was my intent.

It was at this point that I realized I would have to formulate my own course content and sequence, relying on the knowledge and skills I had acquired through workshop training and self-directed study, as well as assistance from my teaching partner, who was equally enthusiastic about the course and who had had graduate level training in clinical improvisation. At this juncture, he and I pooled and reviewed the various resources we had acquired from our own training, including course syllabi, handouts from courses and professional workshops, and notes that we had taken on readings and presentations. We also began creating our own handouts to "fill in the gaps" and to concretize meaningful aspects of our own previous clinical experiences in improvisation.

When the course got off the ground, I began evaluating my decisions about what content to include and in what sequence. I relied dually on my own experiences as the facilitator (sensory, affective, reflective, and intuitive experiences) and on student feedback. The latter manifested as both unsolicited and solicited verbal and written evaluations during class and at the end of each semester. I also sought informal, retrospective feedback from alumni who have taken the course and were practicing in the field. Suggestions from individuals who attended workshops that my teaching partner and I offered at state, regional, and national conferences served as further data for evaluation and revision.

As the years passed, I continued to teach the course, making changes here and there. I also kept vigil for a suitable improvisation textbook. In 2004, Wigram published *Improvisation: Methods and Techniques for Music Therapy Clinicians, Educators and Students* (2004). A few sections of this book have particular relevance for the group improvisation skills that were the focus of the introductory course; however, most of Wigram's writing revolves around tonal constructions on piano and the use of relatively advanced techniques in individual music therapy. What I was looking for was a pedagogical resource that could help me (1) determine which knowledge-based and skill-based competencies my students needed to develop in order to lead effective group improvisation, (2) offer a suggested sequence for training in these competencies, and (3) provide practical exercises toward skill development. With encouragement from others, I decided to write the book I had been searching for.

My interest in forming a course (and eventually writing a book) around skills necessary for the facilitation of group improvisation stems from the notion that in this day and age, most music therapists who practice in this country do not have the luxury of conducting individual therapy sessions exclusively. One reason for this is that group treatment is typically considered more cost-effective than individual treatment by healthcare insurers and treatment agencies. Another reason is that many clients have treatment goals that are accomplished more readily and successfully within a group context. In that the average music therapist will likely be responsible for planning and facilitating group treatment at some point in her or his career, it makes sense that pedagogy and published resources in one of the four fundamental music therapy methods would reflect this expectation.

ESSENTIAL COMPETENCIES

It seems to me that all music therapists, regardless of the clinical populations and ages they serve or the philosophical or theoretical orientations within which they work, require a set of essential competencies in order to effectively lead group improvisation. These competencies are both knowledge-based and skill-based. In other words, therapists must both *know* certain things and *know how to do* certain things. It should be evident that the first set of competencies has to do with the acquisition of information and the latter has to do with the actions that the therapists perform, ideally, as connected to the knowledge that they have acquired.

The American Music Therapy Association (AMTA) and the Certification Board for Music Therapists (CBMT) each designate professional competencies related to improvisation. AMTA includes three broad skills in its document (AMTA, 1999):

8. Improvisation Skills
8.1 Improvise on percussion instruments.
8.2 Compose and develop original melodies, accompaniments, and short pieces extemporaneously in a variety of moods and styles, vocally, and instrumentally.
8.3 Improvise in small ensembles.

Unfortunately, none of these competencies relates to *clinical* music improvisation; there is no mention of clients or therapeutic processes, essential ingredients that define clinical music improvisation and distinguish it from other forms of improvisation, such as jazz. (Detailed definitions of clinical music improvisation and music improvisation appear in Chapter Two.)

The CBMT *Scope of Practice* (2005) offers two items for our consideration, the first under the heading *Music Theory, Perception, and Skills in Clinical Situations:*

> B. Music Skills and Perception
> 4. Improvise music (e.g., vocal, instrumental)

Although the heading indicates that this competency applies to clinical circumstances, there is, again, no mention of clients or therapeutic processes. The second has greater relevance but is just as broad as the others:

> A. Treatment Implementation
> 3. Use methods to achieve therapeutic goals
> h. improvise music to facilitate therapeutic processes

It is my opinion that students and novice therapists need more clear-cut guidance as they prepare to lead clinical improvisation experiences. Among the skill-based competencies, therapists need both nonmusical and musical skills in order to become effective leaders. Simply put, nonmusical competencies include verbal skills and *gestural* actions (movements performed to communicate feeling or intention), while musical skills involve the musical actions that therapists perform. I believe that these two skill sets, nonmusical and musical, function together toward competent facilitation of clinical improvisation.

When I refer to the musical skills that therapists need in order to lead clinical improvisation, I am talking about *clinical music skills*. Implicit here is that the therapists have already developed certain necessary *foundational music skills*—technique, expression, repertoire, etc., on a primary instrument and several additional instruments. The assumption is that therapists can learn to tailor these skills to the therapeutic setting in order to establish and maintain a meaningful relationship with their clients and help these clients progress toward established goals and objectives. Foundational music skills are, for example, what enable therapists to (1) maintain a steady pulse, (2) generate varied rhythmic patterns, (3) modify dynamics, and (4) play an unmetered tremolo, none of which, at face value, have any particular clinical purpose or require any kind of relationship with another player. Clinical music skills, on the other hand, are employed when those same therapists (1) maintain a steady pulse as a way to provide needed constancy for the other players, (2) generate varied rhythmic patterns to discourage unhealthy rigidity and entice novel musical dialogue, (3) modify dynamics in order to model freedom of expression of various feeling states, and (4) play an unmetered tremolo in order to suspend the improvisation while the players switch instruments, reflect on what they have just played, or decide what to play next. In other words, music therapists who have developed clinical music skills are able to create music in an authentic, communicative, flexible, and intentional manner. In this context, *authentic* means with genuineness of expression, *communicative* means with a desire and ability to make meaningful contact with the other players, *flexible* means in a responsive and adaptable manner, and *intentional* means with a clear clinical purpose in mind. It is, perhaps, a combination of these four dimensions that therapists ultimately ought to strive to achieve in their improvisational work.

Darnley-Smith and Patey (2003) write about discerning some of these clinical music abilities in the potential music therapy candidate:

> In addition to playing prepared music, can the player improvise in response to another player? Do they listen to what another might play and respond in the moment? Can they use their voice to sing expressively, even if they might never have had formal training? Of prime importance, music therapists need to feel 'at home' in playing music. It needs to be an integral part of them, both in terms of what they do in their lives and as a natural means of self-expression. This is a relationship which formal training with a certificate can suggest but never guarantee. (p. 57)

It is obvious from my experiences as an educator that some of the most technically or expressively talented students (those who possess solid foundational skills) have great difficulty moving past printed notes on the page in order to reach this kind of personal connection to their authentic "inner music" and its outward communicative power with clients. Does this mean that these individuals have nothing to offer the field of music therapy? Certainly not! It means that they need to work extra hard to find and create opportunities for meaningful connections with their own music-making and a chance to share these experiences with others. I have created some of the exercises in this book to assist in this process, but this is only the beginning. There is always more work to be done. And, while I firmly embrace the value of improvisation as a therapeutic method, when all is said and done, I also recognize that improvisation is not a "good fit" for every music therapist.

In preparing this book, it is my assumption that most undergraduate students (some percussion majors excepted) have not had sufficient foundational training on percussion instruments, even though these are used more often by certified music therapists than other instruments in group-based improvisation (Hiller, 2006). In my experience, although students may have taken a course or two in percussion techniques or percussion pedagogy, unless these courses are taught or informed by music therapy faculty, the focus is almost always on the playing, teaching, and maintenance of symphonic instruments. I sense that this is gradually changing, with the increasing popularity of and media attention to ethnic instruments and their use in a wide variety of musical genres. At present, however, most of the students whom I encounter have had little or no prior training on the percussion instruments common to music therapy improvisation—djembes, congas, bongos, bodhrans, hand-held rhythm instruments, etc. For this reason, I have included rhythm-based foundational music skill exercises in this text, interspersed among exercises that focus upon the use of these skills toward specific clinical aims.

Likewise, although most musicians have had adequate training in identifying and playing conventional Western scales and modes (chromatic, major, and minor) and the harmonies based upon them, the modalities and harmonies used in clinical improvisation reach beyond these to include unconventional tonal constructions. Thus, I have included some tonal-based foundational music skill exercises.

The knowledge-based and skill-based competencies in the book have been created primarily from my own work in the classroom and clinic with undergraduate students. As noted above, I have also relied heavily upon several of the facilitation techniques that appear in Bruscia's "Sixty-Four Clinical Techniques" in *Improvisational Models of Music Therapy* (1987, pp. 533–557). Those that I have chosen to include verbatim from this comprehensive list are music-based techniques that my students and I have found most pertinent to undergraduate pre-clinical and clinical training.

Altogether, the competencies pinpointed in this book fall into three categories: Preparatory Skills, Facilitative Skills, and Verbal Processing Skills. *Preparatory Skills* (PR) refer to those decisions and actions of the therapist that, in some cases, precede the arrival of the players and, in all cases, precede the actual music improvisation. In the "before, during, and after" of improvisation, Preparatory Skills are employed *before the experience*. They revolve around the ability of the therapist to comprehend terms and nomenclature germane to the method (Chapter Two), to manipulate the tools and settings used for improvisation, including musical instruments (Chapter Three) and elements (Chapter Four), and to determine suitable structures for improvisation (Chapter Five).

Facilitative Skills revolve around the ability of the therapist to employ techniques that will elicit a response from the players or shape their immediate experience (Bruscia, 1987). In the "before, during, and after" of improvisation, Facilitation Skills are employed *during the experience*. These skills include the ability to use nonmusical (NM) (Chapter Six) and musical (MU) techniques (Chapter Seven) in order to engage your clients, and being able to listen (LI), comprehend, and describe what is heard (Chapter Eight).

Verbal Processing Skills (VP) refer to those skills required to effectively sort out and verbally process the improvisation experience. In the "before, during, and after" of improvisation, Verbal Processing Skills (Chapter Nine) are employed *after the experience*. These skills help the therapist to recognize and discuss significant aspects of the experience with clients and may assist her or his communication with co-therapists, and/or supervisors.

Specific Preparatory, Facilitative, and Processing competencies are displayed in Appendix A and at the top of certain sections within the chapters that follow, as relevant. (Note: Appendix A can be used as a competency checklist to track ongoing progress.)

SUGGESTIONS FOR USING THIS BOOK

This book contains 80 exercises designed to reinforce competency in the aforementioned areas (see Appendix B). The exercises represent three types of learning that have emerged as invariable aspects of the introductory course that I teach. I term these *Didactic Learning*, *Experiential Learning*, and *Independent Skill Development*. Didactic Learning relates to philosophical, theoretical, and/or practical information that is communicated via lecture, discussion, and modeling. Experiential Learning refers to the students' first-hand experiences in the learning/therapy group process that accompanies didactic instruction. In this form of learning, students have opportunities to observe, participate in, co-lead, lead, and verbally process improvisation experiences. In Independent Skill Development, the third style of learning, students engage in skill-building experiences independently and with partners, outside of the classroom setting.

The exercises for Experiential Learning and Independent Skill Development are meant to serve as a "jumping off point" in the maturity of specific competencies. As such, the reader should feel free to abbreviate, simplify, amplify, or modify the exercises as needed. Repetition of exercises is recommended if time permits.

The book also contains several, diverse clinical vignettes designed to serve as models or challenge the reader to grapple with clinical decisions related to the use of improvisation.

If this book is used as a text for an undergraduate course, it is suggested that students complete reading assignments prior to classroom sessions and that the instructor allow ample time to present the material and answer questions that may arise before proceeding to the practical exercises. It is further recommended that the instructor assume a variety of roles during the group exercises, including observer, facilitator, and participant. The instructor's decision of which part to play, like the therapist's decision in clinical improvisation, will be dependent upon the goal of the exercise and the particular needs, strengths, deficits, and dynamics of the group. Each of these three roles has distinct advantages: Acting as an observer, the instructor is able to perceive "the whole picture" or attend to details that she or he may otherwise miss while engaged in music-making. This role also affords the group an opportunity to work through certain challenges without relying on the certainty of being "rescued" by the leader. Acting as a facilitator, the instructor can direct, model, and provide immediate feedback. Acting as a participant with no leadership responsibilities, the instructor can share in the experience of authentic expression and relate to the other players with more equanimity and intimacy.

I strongly recommend periodic lengthening of appropriate exercises in order to allow for sustained engagement in improvisation. *Sustained engagement* (defined here as improvising in a continuous fashion for more than five minutes) has several distinct benefits. First, players need to build stamina in preparation for leading lengthy group improvisations. Second, the improvisers usually develop confidence and become more expressive as they become increasingly familiar with and trusting of their instruments and the group process. Third, novel musical challenges undoubtedly emerge as time passes, giving the players a chance to employ coping and problem-solving skills. Finally, authentic relationships among the players in a group usually need ample time to emerge and mature.

At the end of each chapter, I have placed a vocabulary list of terms that are considered to be important for review. The instructor and students may use this list as a way to summarize the chapter, to review at the start of each new class session, or to evaluate comprehension and retention on a periodic basis. I have found that repeating a brief group exercise from the previous session and asking students to demonstrate what they have accomplished in their independent skill practice are effective means of starting each new class session. At times, I have asked individual students to begin the session by leading the group in an original exercise that targets a specific competency.

If there are students in the classroom who have advanced musical skills, they may be able to assume a greater leadership role than their peers. For instance, they may take responsibility for starting or stopping the improvisation experiences, providing individual assistance for the players who are having difficulty with certain manipulative skills, creating or adapting group exercises, and/or observing the improvisation experiences and providing verbal feedback. I also have relied on the advanced percussionists to help me keep the instruments tuned and in good working condition.

Vocabulary for Chapter One

1. *Nordoff & Robbins Music Therapy (Creative Music Therapy)*
2. *Gestural*
3. *Foundational Music Skills*
4. *Clinical Music Skills*
5. *Authentic*
6. *Communicative*
7. *Flexible*
8. *Intentional*
9. *Preparatory Skills*
10. *Nonmusical Facilitative Skills*
11. *Musical Facilitative Skills*
12. *Verbal Processing Skills*
13. *Didactic Learning*
14. *Experiential Learning*
15. *Independent Skill Development*
16. *Sustained Engagement*

Chapter Two

TERMS AND NOMENCLATURE OF IMPROVISATION

FOUNDATIONAL DEFINITIONS

Before we make music, let us spend some time learning about the vocabulary of clinical music improvisation. The comprehension of a specific improvisation vocabulary is a desirable knowledge-based preparatory competency, one that permeates all aspects of the work that you will do.

Competencies addressed in this section include the ability to:

PR 1   *Define clinical music improvisation.*
PR 2   *Define and accurately use terms relevant to clinical music improvisation (e.g., method, procedure, technique, referential, nonreferential, etc.)*

An adapted version of Hiller's (2006) definition of *clinical music improvisation* is used in this book:

> Clinical Music Improvisation is the process whereby the therapist and client(s) improvise together for purposes of therapeutic assessment, treatment, and/or evaluation. In clinical improvisation, client and therapist relate to one another through the music, and the improvisation results in a musical product that varies in aesthetic, expressive, and interpersonal significance.

For ease of writing, clinical music improvisation is sometimes referred to herein as *improvisation*. It is understood that this term does not refer to *music improvisation,* which can be defined as follows:

> Music Improvisation is the process whereby the individuals extemporaneously create music while singing or playing. The

intent is most often to produce a musical product of aesthetic value. In music improvisation, the individuals do not relate to one another within a client-therapist relationship, and neither the process nor the outcome is intended to be therapeutic in any way (Hiller, 2006).

Improvisations may be *solo, dyadic, or group*. Solo improvisations involve one player (client or therapist), dyadic involve two players (client and therapist, client and client, therapist and co-therapist), and group involve more than two players (clients or clients and therapists). In group improvisation, then, it is possible to employ solo, dyadic, and group improvisations. The primary focus of this book is group improvisation, in which more than two players are actively engaged in spontaneous music-making at the same time.

The labels *therapist, facilitator,* and *leader* are used synonymously in this text. The terms *clients, improvisers,* and *players* are also used synonymously. Although the therapist typically improvises with her or his clients and thus may be considered an improviser or player, there is here a clear distinction between the person who is primarily responsible for planning and facilitating the experience and the players who are the primary focus or are intended to receive the therapeutic benefits of the improvisation experience.

Throughout this book, you will encounter the terms *effective* and *effectively*. These words can mean many things in many contexts; in this text, these descriptors are employed to refer to outcomes that are successful (toward a particular clinical aim) and to client experiences that are meaningful and/or satisfying in some way.

The term *percussion-based* refers to improvisation that is created with percussive sounds generated on or by the body and on various drums and handheld rhythm instruments. To clarify further, percussion instruments are those that are meant to be beaten with the hands and struck together or with a mallet *(strikers),* shaken *(shakers),* or scraped *(scrapers)*. The term *tonal-based* refers to improvisation that is created with melodies and/or harmonies on tonal instruments. Tonal instruments are those that have the capability to produce distinct pitches to form melodies and harmonies. Examples include piano, guitar, voice, and barred instruments, such as glockenspiels, xylophones, metallophones, and tone bars. I say "have the capability" because the aforementioned tonal instruments can be employed in a percussive fashion; in fact, the piano and barred instruments are considered percussion instruments. Their categorization here thus depends upon how they are used. They are percussive if used in a primarily rhythmic (versus tonal) manner in the improvisation, and they are tonal if used in a primarily melodic or harmonic (versus rhythmic) manner. Of course, in any given improvisation, a tonal instrument may be used in both fashions.

In this book you will find words that are familiar to you but that require definition in an improvisational context. Three such terms are *method, procedure, and technique*. You will also encounter terms that are likely unfamiliar to you, such as *referential, nonreferential, referent,* and *given*. These and other associated terms come from a vocabulary and nomenclature first coined by Bruscia (1987, 1989) and now used and embellished by many practitioners who use improvisation regularly in their work. It is crucial that you have a clear conceptualization of all of these terms so that as you progress through this book, encounter other resources on improvisation, talk about this method with others, and facilitate clinical improvisation experiences, your understanding and discourse will have clarity and integrity.

Clinical music improvisation is practiced according to a number of different models. A music therapy *model* can be considered a comprehensive approach that includes theoretical concepts, clinical indications, goals and objectives, guidelines for implementation, and an explanation of the typical manifestation of the model in actual practice (Bruscia, 1998). Some music therapists align with Nordoff and Robbins (1977), others practice Priestley's Analytical Music Therapy (1975), and still others adhere to a model that is their own unique creation or amalgam. Within each model of improvisation, clinicians use a distinctive vocabulary and nomenclature to communicate about their work. Even a cursory glance through Bruscia's *Improvisational Models of Music Therapy* (1987) will reveal myriad approaches to clinical improvisation and the corresponding vocabularies that have been developed to describe the processes and products of these various models.

Method, Procedure, and Technique

Let us begin this section with a discussion of the terms *method, procedure, and technique*. It is important to do so because often these terms are used synonymously when, in fact, they mean very different things. Each of these concepts is detailed in *Defining Music Therapy* (Bruscia, 1998), so a brief description will suffice in this book. If you do not understand the differences between the concepts after having read this section, I urge you to refer to the original source.

Improvisation is one of four basic music therapy methods. A *method* is a particular type of music experience used for assessment, treatment, and/or evaluation. The four main types of experience are improvising, re-creating (playing and singing precomposed music), composition, and listening. Sometimes, the first three are called *active methods* because in these methods, the clients and therapist are typically involved in the active production of sound forms and music using instruments, the body, and the voice. Active methods stand in contrast to listening or *receptive methods*, in which the clients do not produce the music, but rather act as receivers of and responders to the recorded or live music in the clinical environment. (I wish to note that the word *active* here refers specifically to the clients' relationship to the music-making; during receptive experiences, the clients are active in many ways—cognitively, emotionally, physically, etc.—even though they are not actively producing the music.)

Within each method, there are several ways to design an experience. For instance, in the improvisational method, a therapist might facilitate a vocal improvisation with a single client, whereas another therapist or the same therapist on another day might facilitate a percussion-based improvisation with an entire group of clients. Both experiences are examples of the improvisational method, but each varies from the other in several significant ways. The latter variation, instrumental group improvisation, is the salient focus of this book.

A *procedure* is the sum total of an organized sequence of steps that the therapist develops and implements in order to guide the client(s) through the music experience. For instance, in the individual vocal improvisation mentioned above, the procedure might be as follows: (1) discuss client's emotional state and primary needs, (2) warm up the voice with simple vocal exercises, (3) decide upon a title or theme for the improvisation, (4) determine whether the improvisation will be solo (client only), dyadic (client and therapist), accompanied, or unaccompanied, (5) improvise, and (6) discuss the improvisation.

The final term in this section is *technique*. This word refers to the in-the-moment actions of the therapist used to shape the immediate experience of the client(s). More specifically, these are the verbal, gestural, and musical actions performed by the therapist while the experience is occurring. For example, in group instrumental improvisation, imitating one client's rhythmic patterns is a musical facilitation technique that the therapist may employ for any number of reasons, such as to encourage or validate that client within the larger group. Chapters Six and Seven refer to Nonmusical and Musical Facilitation Techniques, respectively.

Referential and Nonreferential Improvisations

Let us move on to the terms *referential* and *nonreferential*. These terms are not new, nor are they unique to clinical improvisation—we find them in earlier writings about music, visual arts, and other aesthetic pursuits (Meyer, 1956)—but when used in this context, they function as an important system of classification. An improvisation (both its process and product) is either referential or nonreferential.

A *referential improvisation* is one that is created in reference to something other than the music itself for example, an image, title, story, feeling, or work of art. During referential improvisation, meaning is formed from and revolves around the *referent*, which is preselected by the therapist or the clients (Bruscia, 2001). Referential improvisations can also be termed *theme-based* or *programmatic*. The expression *program music* has been used to describe music that attempts to suggest, rather than imitate, sounds in nature (birdsong, water, etc.) or narratives (poetry). I prefer the term *referential* because it seems to imply a broader range of possible subject matter. It also allows for attempts at direct imitation, which is considered undesirable in programmatic music but which could be, at times, a desirable outcome in improvisation.

In contrast to music organized around a referent, sometimes we create *nonreferential improvisations* with our clients. These types of improvisations are created around and derive their meaning from and in relation to the music and sounds themselves. These improvisations are sometimes called *nonprogrammatic* or *free improvisations*. I prefer the term *nonreferential*, primarily because the word *free* may be confused with a particular clinical model attributed to Juliette Alvin, Free Improvisation Therapy (1982), in which no structures whatsoever are imposed upon the clients' improvisations. While some nonreferential improvisations may be truly free, others may be structured through the use of various parameters, or *givens*. The concept of givens will be explored more fully in this and subsequent chapters.

It bears mentioning that with both types of improvisation, referential and nonreferential, different types of meanings may be attributed after the improvisation occurs, as the players ponder and/or discuss it. In hindsight, for example, the players may give meaning to a referential improvisation that does not relate in any way to the pre-established referent (Gardstrom, 2004). Likewise, after a nonreferential improvisation, the players may attach a title, suggesting an internal point of reference (Priestley, 1994), or ascribe symbolic meanings to the improvisation (Bruscia, 2001).

Some referents are considered *static referents* in that the word/concept being portrayed suggests music or sound that does not change considerably over time. Examples of static referents are "sleepy time," "calm," and "a busy city street." Note that static does not refer to the quality of the music itself—a busy street implies loud sounds, a quick tempo, and thick textures—but rather to the sameness of the musical elements over time. A *dynamic referent,* on the other hand, is one that involves musical movement and change from beginning to end. Examples of dynamic referents are "a typical day," "the storm," and "the progression of my illness." Sometimes referents are used in tandem with one another as a guide for shifting from the representation of one concept to its opposite. Examples of such *continuum referents* are "anxious to calm" and "denial to acceptance." Continuum referents are always dynamic, in that the music changes as players move from one end of the continuum to the other. Appendix C contains further examples of static, dynamic, and continuum referents that may have utility in clinical improvisation.

Ex 2–1 (Experiential) Optional

If members of the group already have a functional understanding of the instruments of improvisation (see Chapter Three), play through several of the static and dynamic referents in Appendix C. Discuss the outcomes.

As the therapist moves through all phases of an improvisation experience, from planning to evaluating, she or he will encounter both *process* and *product,* two dimensions of improvisation that are inextricably linked. In short, process refers to the manner in which the improvisation unfolds, or the "how" of the experience (who plays what, in what manner, when, and with whom), and the *product* is the actual music that results from that process of unfolding, or the "what" of the experience. The juxtaposition of the dimensions of "how" and "what" with the dimensions of referential and nonreferential makes for countless combinations of action and sound. Let us explore a few scenarios.

As noted, a referential improvisation flows from, is guided by, and derives meaning in relationship to an external referent. Using sounds and music, the players strive to symbolize that referent. At times this process happens individually, even within group treatment, with each player's attention turned toward the referent and the degree to which her or his own playing matches her or his concept of the referent. In this case, each improviser's focus is on her or his own playing, rather than on the actions of the other individual players or on the total group process. As you may imagine, at times the product that results from this kind of process sounds more like a collection of concurrent individual improvisations, similar yet unrelated. This reminds me of what someone would hear during a stroll through an open air market, in which each of the street vendors cries out for the same purpose, yet where each cry is distinctive from and somewhat misaligned with the next.

In contrast, there are times when a group rallies collectively around a referent and the result is a highly unified and sophisticated musical product. This may occur, for example, when the members have a strong sense of group identity because they have played together frequently or over a long period of time. Even in fledgling groups, particularly when members have lived through common hardships (cancer, death of a spouse, physical abuse, suicide, mental illness, etc.), intimate relationships can develop quickly. In these cases, each player may give more attention to the other players, and the musical product resulting from this attentive process may sound more cohesive.

Notice that I say "this may occur." This is because group cohesiveness is neither a surefire guarantee of nor a prerequisite for a cohesive process or product. There are many other factors that enter into the equation. One such factor is the specific referent applied to the improvisation. This structural device has a bearing upon both process and product. Consider, for example, the word "disengaged" versus the word "solidarity" or the continuum referent "our family, before and after treatment." With the first referent, one would expect the improvisers to play in a disconnected manner resulting in disconnected sounds; in the latter instances, the themes themselves suggest that the group members would attempt to work more closely together in order to represent the referent, listening and responding to one another's music in a concerted fashion.

The process of releasing and providing relief from conscious or unconscious (repressed) feelings is called *catharsis*. Cathartic expression can occur during instrumental improvisation; the resulting product is called an expressive *sound form*. (The word "form" here refers to an entity, not an ordered pattern.) For example, consider three siblings who are depicting their feelings of rage toward someone who has abused or betrayed them. What emerges is a very loud piece without a constant or predictable pulse, without a cohesive melody or harmony, and without a distinguishable overarching plan. The authentic outpouring of profound psychological material, such as feelings of rage, is often emancipated from the conventional rhythmic, tonal, and formal structures that typify music and distinguish it from sound.

Givens

In this final section of the chapter, I will share a definition of the term *given* and describe three specific types. A parameter or given (Bruscia, 1987) can be considered a structure, limit, or consideration for the improvisation. It "serves to direct the group's attention" and "provides the players with a common focus around which to interact" (p. 175).

Wigram (2004) uses the term *play rules* to describe the concept of givens, writing,

> Most of all, play rules are structured in order to give some sort of sense of meaning and direction to the improvisational experiences that are going on, either at a purely musical level or at the more therapeutic level where musical improvisation is applied in clinical work. They can add a dimension of containment, safety and security to an experience that may well feel both challenging and unsafe for the client(s). (p. 41)

It should be obvious that a referent is a type of given or play rule, as its very purpose is to provide a structure and focus for the group's music-making. However, as we shall see, there are other types of givens that may be used singularly or in combination to structure both referential and nonreferential improvisations.

Bruscia outlines three types of givens that may assist the group in focusing the improvisation: vocabulary, procedural, and interpersonal. *Vocabulary givens* are those parameters related to the number or sorts of sounds that may be used by the players, including what instruments may be played and in what manner. An example of a vocabulary given is the specification that only instruments played with mallets be used. *Procedural givens,* as the name implies, relate to aspects of improvisation procedure, and often guide the timing (sequence or length) of events within the piece. An example of a procedural given is the mandate that a group of players improvise continuously for no less than eight minutes. *Interpersonal givens* are used to specify the types of relationships that are created between the players, either prior to the improvisation or as it unfolds. An example of an interpersonal given is the directive to play in particular dyads within the group. The reader is referred to Bruscia's *Improvisational Models of Music Therapy* (1987) for more detailed information about these three types of parameters as well as considerations for their selection and implementation.

Givens, including referents, may be established by the therapist or the members of the group, depending on a variety of factors. They may be based upon a preconceived plan of action or an immediate need that arises during the session. Oftentimes, the group members or therapist will select a referent for an improvisation in response to the preceding improvisation. You will gain practice in determining suitable givens for group improvisation as you work through the various exercises in this book.

Improvisation Versus a Drum Circle

It is critical that you understand the distinction between clinical improvisation and a *drum circle*. The two experiences are often mistaken for one another, even though they are more different than alike. Reread the definition of Clinical Music Improvisation that appears at the beginning of this chapter. (Do it now!) Contrast this with the following description of a drum circle, excerpted from the website of Arthur Hull (2006), considered by many to be the "father" of community drum circles:

> A drum circle is "the use of a rhythm based event as a tool for unity...a collaboratively, self-organized and musical event created 'in the moment' by all the people who participate" and a means of "expressing timeless joy, passion, and release through the power of rhythm."

You can see right away that there are similarities between community drumming and percussion-based group improvisation. Both experiences involve groups of people making music together, and both are oriented around drums and other rhythm instruments. However, each centers on different purposes, materials, processes, role relationships, and outcomes. Table 1, below, may help you make a side-by-side comparison of the two experiences. Perhaps most importantly, improvisation is geared around individualized needs as determined through assessment, whereas the primary intent of a drum circle is to promote social unity and personal enjoyment through rhythm-based playing. You are encouraged to visit the aforementioned website and others like it in order to increase your awareness.

Table 1
A comparison of features of clinical music improvisation and a drum circle

	Improvisation	Drum Circle
Purpose/Aim	Oriented around growth and development in functional domains (social, emotional, communicative, physical, etc.)	Oriented around social and recreational aims (building a sense of community, sharing rhythm, having fun)
	Based on individualized assessment and planning	No basis in formal, individualized assessment or planning
Materials	Include all instruments, voice, body sounds	Include drums and handheld percussion instruments
	Referential or nonreferential	Nonreferential
	Rhythmic or arrhythmic	Rhythmic
Processes	Musical or musical and verbal	Musical
	Intrapersonal and interpersonal	Somewhat intrapersonal, but primarily interpersonal
	Structured or unstructured	Highly structured
	Processes shaped by therapeutic aims	Processes shaped by social and recreational aims
	Documented	Not documented
Roles and Relationships	Clients have personal disability, illness, or special need	Clients do not necessarily have a personal disability, illness or special need
	Group members are typically homogeneous	Participants are typically heterogeneous
	Facilitator is a MT-BC	Facilitator is not typically a MT-BC

	Facilitator may be directive or nondirective	Facilitator is directive
	Facilitator establishes personal relationship with clients	Facilitator does not establish relationship with individual participants
	Facilitator uses techniques to accomplish therapeutic aims	Facilitator uses techniques to accomplish social and recreational aims
	Clients respond to inherent challenges and play within established givens	Participants respond to and play within "fundamental groove" (Hull, 2006)
	Clients abide by unique "rules" established within the improvisation group	Participants abide by accepted "drum circle etiquette" (Hull, 2006)
Outcomes	Progress toward individual and collective goals and objectives	Progress toward a sense of community, enjoyment
	Musical product may or may not be heard as aesthetically pleasing	Musical product is typically heard as aesthetically pleasing
	Periodically evaluated	Not formally evaluated

Vocabulary for Chapter Two

1. *Clinical Music Improvisation*
2. *Music Improvisation*
3. *Solo Improvisation*
4. *Dyadic Improvisation*
5. *Group Improvisation*
6. *Therapist/Facilitator/Leader*
7. *Clients/Improvisers/Players*
8. *Effective/Effectively*
9. *Percussion-based*

10.   *Strikers*
11.   *Shakers*
12.   *Scrapers*
13.   *Model*
14.   *Method*
15.   *Procedure*
16.   *Technique*
17.   *Referential*
18.   *Referent*
19.   *Programmatic*
20.   *Theme-based*
21.   *Nonreferential*
22.   *Nonprogrammatic*
23.   *Free*
24.   *Static Referent*
25.   *Dynamic Referent*
26.   *Continuum Referent*
27.   *Process*
28.   *Product*
29.   *Catharsis*
30.   *Sound Form*
31.   *Givens*
32.   *Play Rules*
33.   *Vocabulary Givens*
34.   *Procedural Givens*
35.   *Interpersonal Givens*
36.   *Drum Circle*

Chapter Three

INSTRUMENTS OF IMPROVISATION

INSTRUMENTARIUM

Competencies addressed in this section include the ability to:

PR 3   Identify by name all instruments in the improvisation instrumentarium.

As you prepare to lead group improvisation, you will need to gain access to a wide variety of instruments. If, like many music therapists, you are traveling to your clients in hospitals, schools, nursing homes, clinics, community centers, etc., the instruments you select will need to be portable. This means that you will have a combination of drums, hand-held rhythm instruments, and barred melodic instruments. You may also find use for an electronic keyboard, guitar, or any number of woodwind, string, or brass instruments, depending upon your client configuration, their clinical goals and objectives, and your treatment setting. If you are fortunate enough to have a "home base" for treatment sessions, you may have access to larger instruments, such as a piano or trap set. (The human voice, a powerful tool in clinical improvisation, is not specifically addressed in this text.) Your unique collection of percussion and tonal instruments is called your *instrumentarium*.

Table 2 below contains a generous array of percussion and tonal instruments suitable for clinical improvisation with a range of individuals and for a multiplicity of clinical aims. Most of these instruments can be found at music stores in urban areas or online through any number of reputable music merchants.

Mallets

It is important to mention that your experience of playing percussion instruments (and your clients' experiences) will differ considerably depending upon whether you are using your hands or mallets. Mallets serve as an extension of your hands and, thus, an extension of the movements you are producing. Different mallet lengths and heads produce different sensations and sound outcomes. It is worth your time to experiment with the differences between hand and mallet playing with all of the exercises in this chapter and those in subsequent chapters.

When using two mallets with novice players, I recommend *matched grip* rather than traditional grip. Matched grip involves holding both mallets in the same fashion, between the first joint of the index finger with the other fingers wrapped loosely around the shaft of the mallet. Matched grip is sometimes termed "bicycle grip" in that it resembles the way one holds the handles of a bicycle, with the backs of the hands facing upward. The stroke is identical in the left and right hands, and consists of a natural down-up motion.

Occasionally, you will encounter clients who have trained with *traditional grip* and prefer it to a matched style. Traditional grip, used in some marching bands, involves holding the right stick as in matched grip and the shaft of the left mallet under the thumb and between the second and third fingers. The strokes of the left and right hand are not identical; the left stroke involves a sideways motion of the wrist, which many players may find awkward and difficult to control.

Getting to Know Your Instruments

Once you have established an instrumentarium, it is critical that you become intimately familiar with every piece in your collection. This means first learning what to call each of them. (I have a distressing memory of a rather ill-prepared and anxious student who, when introducing the instruments to a group of adults in a psychiatric hospital, referred to the cabasa as "this shaky thing-a-ma-bob." It occurred to me at the time that this was a fair description of the student herself!) I prefer that our students use proper musical terminology with their clients, rather than slang terms or simplified names. If a child has difficulty saying or recalling the proper name of an instrument, however, it may be prudent to simplify, as long as the new name is used consistently during the sessions and, if possible, in other environments in which the child encounters that same instrument. If you choose a new name, use one that somehow relates to the sound of the instrument, the manner in which it is played, or the way it looks, in order that it become more memorable. I may refer to maracas as "*s*hakers," for example, or claves as "click sticks." With adults who have typical verbal functioning, there should be no need to alter the names of the instruments, but clients may need their memories jogged prior to the improvisation.

You must also learn a bit about the history of each instrument, how it feels to play it, the various ways it can be sounded (playing configuration), and the unique physical challenges that it presents. Learning about the instruments in your instrumentarium will take considerable time and practice, but this kind of knowledge and skill with your professional "tools of the trade" is absolutely imperative. When students question why music therapists spend so much time and effort developing performance skills, I remind them that we have to be competent enough on the various instruments of improvisation that we can, in a sense, forget about our own playing so as to focus our attention squarely upon the client.

Ambidexterity

While we are discussing performance skill, and before we launch into the first rhythmic exercise, let me mention that as a facilitator, you ought to strive toward *ambidexterity* with the instruments, that is, the ability to use your left and right hands with equal ease and expertise. There are a number of reasons for this. One is that sometimes you will need to demonstrate rhythmic patterns involving extensive use of one arm/hand or the other, especially if you are trying to encourage the use of a particular side of the body. At other times you will need to model for players who are seated across from you. In this case, if the client intends to play Right-Left-Right-Right (*R-L-R-R),* you will need to play Left-Right-Left-Left (*L-R-L-L*) in mirror fashion. Another reason for developing ambidexterity is that it frequently becomes necessary to conduct the group or physically assist a client while continuing to play (see Chapter Six). If that client happens to be seated on your dominant side, the nondominant arm/hand may be pressed into action. Finally, there will most certainly be times when one of your arms or hands is fatigued and you must rest while continuing to play with the other.

In order to develop ambidexterity, anytime you play the exercises in this book, be sure to explore a variety of Left-Right (*L-R*) configurations.

Ex 3–1 (Independent Skill Development)

Set aside ample and uninterrupted time to examine the instruments one by one. Start with the one that appeals most to your senses. Look carefully at its shape; what does it remind you of? Hold the instrument, and notice the way it feels in your hands and/or against your body. Consider the instrument as an extension of your body, and play it accordingly, with as natural a movement as possible. Experiment with so-called "conventional" and "unconventional" playing techniques. Explore the instrument's dynamic range, from barely audible to barely tolerable.

Note: You may use Table 2 below to complete this exercise, describing some unconventional techniques and commenting on anything you find to be significant about each instrument.

Table 2
Suggested (Portable) Instrumentarium for Group Improvisation

Instrument	Unconventional Playing Techniques	Comments
1. Agogo Bells		
2. Bodhran		
3. Bongos		
4. Cabasa		
5. Chime Tree		
6. Chromatic Bells		
7. Claves		
8. Conga		

9. Cowbell		
10. Crash Cymbal		
11. Cymbal on Stand		
12. Djembe		
13. Doumbek		
14. Egg Shakers		
15. Finger Cymbals		
16. Frame Drum		
17. Ganza		
18. Gathering Drum		
19. Gong		
20. Guiro		
21. Jingle Bells		
22. Maracas		
23. Ocean Drum		
24. Paddle Drum		
25. Rainstick		
26. Rhythm Sticks		

27. Sandblocks		
28. Shekeré		
29. Slit Drum		
30. Snare Drum		
31. Talking Drum		
32. Tambourine		
33. Temple Blocks		
34. Tom-toms		
35. Triangle		
36. Tubano		
37. Woodblock		
38. Wristbells		
37. Alto Metallophone		
38. Soprano Glockenspiel		
39. Alto Xylophone		
40. Tone Bar		
41.		

Ex 3–2 (Independent Skill Development)

Now that you have examined the look and feel of the instruments and various ways to manipulate them, revisit each one and consider its characteristic timbre(s) more fully. Again, start with the one that appeals the most to you. What does its sound remind you of? Can you find a word or phrase to describe this sound?

I often use the following structure with groups of clients who are discovering the instruments of improvisation for the first time. I find it to be a helpful introductory experience because it allows each person to explore the sound possibilities of every instrument in the circle, while also demanding a bit of interaction among the players.

Ex 3–3 (Experiential Learning)

Sit in a circle, each player with a different instrument, if possible. Designate a leader who will sit outside of the circle (or in the very center) and establish a steady beat. Join in with your own rhythms and continue to improvise with the beat until the leader breaks from pulse and plays a rhythmic figure to signal a change. At this point, pass your instrument to the person on your right and accept a new instrument from the person on your left. Listen for the leader's return to pulse, and continue the sequence until all players have sounded all instruments in the circle. Afterward, discuss which instrument(s) you preferred, which were easiest and most difficult to play, etc.

SELECTING THE INSTRUMENTS

Competencies addressed in this section include the ability to:

PR 4   Select instruments for the improvisation experience based upon knowledge and perception of the players' attributes, needs, and clinical objectives.

Now you are ready to learn about instrument selection. First, let us discuss some general guidelines for the selection of instruments. No matter who your clients are or what their attributes may be, I can not stress how important it is to give careful consideration to the structural and aesthetic quality, number, and specific types of instruments that you make available for group improvisation. A nonchalant approach to these decisions could lead to any number of detrimental outcomes, some of which I have witnessed. A lack of quality in construction, for instance, will likely affect client participation. No one wants to play something that appears shabby or produces a displeasing sound! Too few instruments could result in client frustration, because options dwindle as successive group members make their selections or worse, because someone is left without an instrument to play. A dearth of preferred instruments among the selection could lead to resistance, and a lack of variety could restrict client musical and emotional expression.

Quality

Unfortunately, there are therapists who use substandard instruments in their clinical improvisation. Two specific examples include the use of poorly constructed or homemade instruments that produce a meager or inauthentic sound and the employment of children's instruments ("frog" maracas, mini tubano, etc.) with adults. Each and every instrument you offer to a client for the purpose of improvising should be matched to that player's attributes and should be of the highest-quality construction, appearance, and, most importantly, sound. Well-constructed instruments tend to be more durable and predictable over time. Perhaps most importantly, the investment in well-manufactured instruments conveys an attitude of respect for one's self as a professional, for the client as a musical human being, and for the music itself.

Suitable instruments for clinical improvisation may be electric or acoustic; acoustic instruments may be orchestral (tympani, glockenspiel, etc.) or ethnic. Ethnic instruments typically originate in Africa (talking drum, djembe, etc.), Latin America (claves, maracas, etc.), or Asia and the Middle East (gong, doumbek, etc.).

Number

Like every other clinical decision you make as you prepare for improvisation experiences, the number of instruments you provide for the players depends first and foremost upon the clinical aim. In general, however, try to allow for one-and-a-half to two instruments per player. Thus, in a group of 7 clients and one therapist, you would need to provide from 12 to 16 instruments (not necessarily 12 to 16 different types of instruments; there could be some duplication). This amount would allow each person to have a reasonable variety from which to choose, and, depending on the givens established for the improvisation (see Chapter Two), some players could select multiple instruments to use simultaneously within a single experience.

Types

Here again, the types of instruments you provide should be selected with the clinical aim in mind. For example, if you intend to lead the players through an improvisation based on the theme "anger" in order to clarify that emotion, consider the characteristic sounds and actions associated with this emotion. Will the instruments you have chosen allow for the natural expression of anger? Moreover, if you ask your players to look at one another during the improvisation, have you included instruments that can be played without constant visual tracking?

I have noticed that clients who have never before improvised tend to gravitate toward percussion instruments and avoid tonal instruments. This may be because the clients perceive percussion instruments as somehow more accessible than tonal instruments. There is some validity to this perception. In general, drums, and handheld rhythm instruments require less musical knowledge, experience, and skill than melodic or harmonic instruments; they are simply organized and simply manipulated so that the clients can have immediate success in sounding them. I say "in general" because there are tonal instruments that are quite simple to manipulate and with which clients can experience immediate success, if immediate success is an important dimension of the work. Examples include the Orff® barred instruments, Autoharp®, Omnichord®, and certain electronic keyboards.

Of course—and this is a theme that runs throughout this book—clinical decisions are always made on the basis of multiple factors. It is impossible to provide an instrumental recipe for success in all circumstances! Although percussion instruments may be readily accessible, their exclusive use may cause a client to be or feel musically restricted. In Chapter Four we will learn that rhythmic elements primarily relate to the amount or level of energy or force in a player's expressions. Tonal elements (melody and harmony), on the other hand, allow the player to reveal more specific aspects of the quality or direction of that expression. A client's self-expression may thus be fuller and richer with the addition of tonal instruments to the session instrumentarium.

In selecting instruments for group improvisation, particularly as it applies to a heterogeneous group, strive for (1) flexibility of use (portability, compatibility), (2) dynamic capabilities (wide range of loudness levels), (3) variety of timbre (diversity of tone colors), and (4) role possibilities (one player, multiple players, leadership) (Stephens, 1985). Another possible rule of thumb is to provide instruments from three distinct categories of movement. These categories were defined in Chapter Two: (1) *strikers*—those that are beaten with the hands (djembe, bongos, etc.) or struck together or with a mallet (chromatic bells, woodblock, claves, etc.), (2) *shakers*—those that are shaken (maracas, shakere, etc.), and (3) *scrapers*—those whose surfaces are scraped (cabasa, guiro, etc.). When each of these categories of movement is represented, I find that the instrumentarium typically embodies diversity in dynamic and timbral potential as well. Now we will move on to specific client attributes and objectives.

Client Age

I have already alluded to the fact that age is an important consideration in selecting instruments for improvisation. As stated above, it is recommended that you use "adult" (professionally constructed and full-sized) instruments for adult players. Try to apply this guideline to all adults, no matter what their level of cognitive functioning. In my opinion, it is no more appropriate to use children's instruments with an adult who has mental retardation, brain injury, or dementia than it is to sing children's songs, such as "Mary Had a Little Lamb" or "I'm a Little Teapot!" I also recommend adult instruments for teenagers. Bear in mind that some instruments may be too heavy for elderly clients.

Although the period of adolescence is characterized by unpredictable wavering between childlike and adult behaviors, I have found that adolescent clients prefer to be treated as adults during music-making endeavors. Additionally, with individuals between the ages of 12 and 18, it is important to provide instruments that are "fashionable," that is, the types of instruments that are associated with the performers whom adolescents admire. In my experience, teenagers involved in improvisation tend to gravitate toward all manner of drums (Gardstrom, 2004), as well as guitars, keyboards, and certain handheld Latin percussion instruments such as tambourines and maracas.

Typically developing children have smaller hands and less manual dexterity than adolescents or adults. For this reason, I sometimes use instruments that are manufactured for younger players. For example, plastic egg shakers are preferred to traditional maracas because the eggs are lighter, smaller, and easier to control. Drums with large heads provide an easier target than those with smaller heads. With very young children, I recommend freestanding instruments (floor toms, gathering drums, mini-tubanos) over those that must be held, balanced, or manipulated on a lap while the child attempts to sound them. For this reason, commercially prepared stands for instruments such as djembes and triangles are a good investment. Short mallets and those with wide handles or bolster cuffs provide for greater success. Young children seem to have the most difficulty coordinating small, two-handed instruments in which each hand is performing a disparate motion. Examples include the agogo bells, finger cymbals, triangle (without a stand), claves, talking drum, tambourine, and cabasa. While neither particularly difficult to hold nor to manipulate, the ocean drum produces a sound that is difficult to control and often perceived as hurtful to small, sensitive ears. For these reasons, the ocean drum is not suggested for improvisation with children. Personally, I do not consider the sandblocks to be a musical instrument; thus I do not use them in improvisation. However, sandblocks are included in the list in Table 2 because some children seem to enjoy playing them, manipulating them can promote the development of purposeful bilateral movement patterns, and they are often included in commercially prepared children's instrument collections that you may purchase. If you do use sandblocks with children, be sure the knobs are a good shape and size for grasping.

If your clients have physical disabilities that prevent the conventional use of instruments, explore the possibility of purchasing adapted instruments. Many merchants now sell apparatuses such as clave and tambourine stands (for one-hand playing) and raised drums with nonstick feet (for wheelchair trays).

Cautions

While we are on the subject of sandblocks, it bears mentioning that some instruments and accessories that are used in clinical improvisation are potentially hazardous to clients, especially to young children. The staples or tacks used to affix sandpaper to the blocks or heads to the drums and tambourines can come loose and injure the player. The elastic straps used to suspend finger cymbals and triangles, mallet heads, and guitar picks are small enough to swallow. In addition, some rainsticks are made from cacti and have residual spines and rough spots that can hurt tender hands.

Needs and Objectives

Along with consideration for age, you will need to select instruments according to client needs and clinical goals and objectives. These are, of course, determined through careful assessment in a variety of functioning domains. Once again, however, there are some general guidelines.

Musical instruments are an extension of the human body. As such, at the most fundamental level, players must be able to move their bodies (sometimes with assistance) to produce and manipulate sound. An astute facilitator will have a sense of each client's *motor functioning* and will provide instruments matched to this functioning level. Thus, it is not enough for you simply to know how to produce sound on each instrument; it is also crucial that you have a clear understanding of the inherent physical challenges of sounding each instrument. If improvisation is indicated as a method to promote changes in motor functioning, that is, increase strength or endurance, improve coordination or dexterity, and increase flexibility or range of motion, the instruments provided for the improvisation should reflect these aims.

Ex 3–4 (Didactic Learning)

Work together to place each instrument listed in Table 2 into one of three piles on the floor: strikers, shakers, or scrapers. (Note: Some instruments may fit into more than one category.) Improvise briefly with the instruments of each subgroup and discuss the specific physical demands required.

The following vignette is designed to help you think through the factors that are important in choosing instruments for one particular client group. Notice that the first question relates to age, the second to client preference, and the remaining to need and clinical goals and objectives.

Vignette 3–1

Imagine that you are working with a 65-year-old man who has hemiplegia (the result of a stroke) and his family. Suppose that his aims are to increase strength and improve coordination in his affected arm (left), and, furthermore, that he has expressed an interest in instrumental improvisation. You have brought with you a small subset from your full instrumentarium. Which instruments might be best matched to this situation? Your sequential decision-making process might go something like this:

1. *Which instruments might I eliminate due to the age of the client and his family members? (too childish: mini tubano, children's floor tom, sandblocks…)*

2. *Of those remaining, are there any instruments that the client or a family member has expressed an interest in playing? (preferred: none, although the client's wife mentioned that her husband has played drums and other rhythm instruments in the past…)*

3. *Of the drums and rhythm instruments, which would require or encourage the use of both of the client's arms? (two-handed instruments: agogo, cabasa, cowbell, frame drum/paddle drum with a mallet, talking drum, triangle…)*

4. *Of the drums and rhythm instruments, which would require or encourage the desired amount of strength? (desired strength: frame drum/paddle drum with mallet in left hand, talking drum…)*

5. *Of these, which instruments would require or encourage the desired amount of coordination? (desired coordination: frame drum/paddle drum with mallet in left hand, talking drum…)*

Of course, there are countless other factors that may enter your decision-making process and affect the outcome. These "what ifs" are hard to predict, yet they are a certainty of clinical work. What if the client in this scenario does not like the sound of the instruments? What if he can not express what he needs to? What if his wife complains that she can not hear the drums very well? What if the client experiences pain while playing? What if...?

As you continue to ponder the inherent physical challenges of each instrument, examine Tables 3 and 4 below.

Table 3
Strength/Endurance
(Note: Top to bottom indicates least to most strength/endurance required.)

STRIKERS	SHAKERS	SCRAPERS
Gathering drum	Wrist bells	Guiro
Chime tree	Egg shakers	Sandblocks
Tubano	Maracas	Cabasa
Cymbal on stand	Jingle bells	
Gong	Rainstick	
Tom-toms	Ocean drum	
Snare drum	Ganza	
Slit drum	Tambourine	
Barred instruments		
Claves		
Temple blocks		
Rhythm sticks		
Frame drum		
Tambourine		
Cowbell		
Woodblock		
Agogo bells		
Paddle drum		
Bodhran		
Triangle		

Finger cymbals		
Crash cymbals		
Conga		
Bongos		
Djembe		
Doumbek		
Talking drum		

Table 4
Coordination/Dexterity
(Note: Top to bottom indicates least to most coordination/dexterity required.)

STRIKERS	SHAKERS	SCRAPERS
Chime tree	Wrist bells	Sandblocks
Gathering drum	Rainstick	Guiro
Tubano	Ocean drum	Cabasa
Djembe	Ganza	
Doumbek	Egg shakers	
Conga	Maracas	
Bongos	Jingle bells	
Gong	Tambourine	
Cymbal on stand		
Tom-toms		
Crash cymbals		
Rhythm sticks		
Paddle drum		
Snare drum		
Temple blocks		
Slit drum		
Frame drum		
Bodhran		
Tambourine		
Woodblock		
Cowbell		
Claves		

Talking drum		
Triangle		
Finger cymbals		
Agogo bells		
Barred instruments		

These tables contain rankings of several percussion instruments along the dimensions of Strength/Endurance and Coordination/Dexterity. (By the way, you can use the categories in these tables to check your responses in *Exercise 3–4*. How did you do?) *Strength/Endurance* refers to the force of a movement required to produce a sound, and the energy that it takes to sustain the sound producing movement over time. *Coordination/Dexterity* relates to the organization of gross and fine muscle groups required to sound the instrument. These rankings are neither precise nor absolute, because the particular demands of an instrument depend somewhat on how it is played, as well as its size and weight. Perhaps you will agree with these rankings, or perhaps your opinion will differ. What is most important is that you learn to keep these dimensions in the forefront of your clinical decision-making.

Ex 3–5 (Independent Skill Development)

With a partner, gather as many of the instruments that appear in Tables 3 and 4 to which you have access. Move down each column (strikers, shakers, and scrapers), playing the instruments in sequence and discussing how they might have achieved their rankings. For example, why might a gathering drum take less strength/endurance to play than a conga drum? Why might a rainstick require less coordination/dexterity than a tambourine? Do you agree or disagree with the rankings? Be prepared to discuss your findings with the entire group.

Certainly, in addition to motor functioning, there are other clinical domains to consider when selecting instruments. For example, therapists often use improvisation as a method to support the emotional lives of their clients, through self-expression, validation, and exploration. As we consider emotional expression, we need to ask an important question: Do some instruments have more expressive potential than others? If by *expressive potential* we are referring to a range of dynamic, timbral, and textural/role capabilities, we can say with certainty that some instruments are indeed more inherently "expressive." That is, by virtue of the way they are constructed, they are able to be sounded in a multiplicity of ways so that the player has more options for self-expression. Table 5 is a ranking of percussion instruments with respect to this dimension of *Sound Variability*.

Table 5
Sound Variability
(Note: Top to bottom indicates least to most variable.)

STRIKERS	SHAKERS	SCRAPERS
Claves	Jingle bells	Sandblocks
Woodblock	Wrist bells	Guiro
Rhythm sticks	Egg shakers	Cabasa
Crash cymbals	Maracas	
Paddle drum	Rainstick	
Chime tree	Ganza	
Cowbell	Tambourine	
Agogo Bells	Ocean drum	
Triangle		
Gong		
Finger cymbals		
Tom-toms		
Tambourine		
Snare drum		
Frame drum		
Bodhran		
Gathering drum		
Bongos		
Conga		
Cymbal on stand		
Slit drum		
Temple blocks		
Doumbek		
Talking drum		

Tubano		
Djembe		
Barred instruments		

Ex 3–6 (Independent Skill Development)

In dyads or triads, as with Exercise 3–5, gather the instruments that appear in Table 5 and play them in sequence. Discuss with one another how each instrument might have achieved its ranking with respect to sound variability. For example, what makes a slit drum inherently more variable than claves? Be prepared to discuss your findings with the entire group.

The following case example will illustrate the juxtaposition of several general and specific factors (such as age, physical abilities, and the clinical objective of promoting emotional expression) in the selection of instruments for another particular group.

Vignette 3–2

Imagine you are working with a group of children, ages 6 to 10, who are being treated in a day clinic for leukemia and other blood disorders. You provide individual and family sessions during medical procedures in the morning and a group session for all children in the afternoon. The children in the group experience fatigue, nausea, pain, or anxiety, and some are strapped to an IV for blood transfusions or chemotherapy during the session. The main clinical aims for the members of the group are to provide for normalization (offering structure and opportunities for socialization), to promote the expression of feelings related to the clients' illnesses and treatment, and to decrease anxiety related to medical procedures and the treatment environment.

Here, the line of questioning might proceed as follows:

1.   *Which instruments might I eliminate due to the age of the clients? (too large or physically demanding: large djembe…)*

2.   *Which instruments might I eliminate as I consider the clients' fatigue (none)*

3.   *Which instruments might I eliminate as I consider the clients' nausea? (none)*

4.   *Which instruments might I eliminate as I consider the clients' pain and anxiety (timbre too harsh: cymbal, gong, ocean drum, shakeré...)*

5.   *Which instruments might I eliminate as I consider those clients who have restricted or no use of one arm (two-handed instruments: agogo bells, claves, cowbell, doumbek, finger cymbals, guiro, paddle drum, rhythm sticks, sandblocks). Note: Some of these two-handed instruments, such as agogo bells, cowbell, doumbek, guiro, paddle drum, and rhythm sticks, could be included if the clients were to play in dyads; in fact, this would support the clinical aim of socialization.*

6.   *Which instruments might best enhance the clients' expressions of emotion? This question is a bit tricky. Obviously, the clients' feelings about their illness and treatment will vary tremendously due to factors such as age at onset, severity of illness, frequency and intensity of treatment, familial support, etc. So, although the claves or wristbells may be perceived as restricting expression, they may actually be the preferred instruments to express the restrictiveness and resulting frustration and boredom that certain clients feel! If, on the other hand, a very specific theme is chosen as a basis for the group improvisation (everyone plays the referent "anger" or "peace"), it may be prudent to eliminate certain instruments and retain others on the basis of the relationship between their sound quality and intensity and the referent being portrayed.*

The Therapist's Instrument

You now have an elementary understanding of some of the factors that need to be considered as you select instruments for clinical improvisation.

In addition to those that you select for the clients, you must also consider the instrument or instruments that you will play in your role as the leader. As Towse and Roberts point out (in Davies & Richards, 2002), the use of the piano or the therapist's "own instrument" (primary instrument of study) in the context of group improvisation can create an unwanted rift. The authors caution:

> Additionally, the use of an instrument not available to the rest of the group will have a significant impact on the dynamic matrix of the group. It may be making the statement, 'I am different from you. I can do something you cannot.' This is not quite the same as the unspoken statement of the group analyst, which is one of 'I am like you but here I have a particular role.' (p. 259)

Again, there is no recipe; most important is that you recognize that even this seemingly benign decision may have a profound impact on the products and processes of group improvisation. Sometimes you will have a specific reason for selecting a given instrument, such as its volume capabilities, its timbre, its associative value, and so forth. At other times, you will wait for the other players to choose their instruments before choosing yours so that the clients will have full access to all of the tools of self-expression.

The following exercise provides an opportunity for you to turn your newly gained knowledge about instrument selection into action.

Ex–7 (Experiential Learning)

Take turns selecting a suitable array of instruments for 6 players with the attributes described below. If helpful, use the rankings in Tables 3, 4, and 5 to inform your decisions:

a.   *adults who have limited grasp and strength due to cerebral palsy*
b.   *school-aged children who are partially sighted and blind*
c.   *adolescents who have severe behavior disorders*
d.   *older adults who have mild to moderate hearing loss*

ARRANGING THE ENVIRONMENT

Competencies addressed in this section include the ability to:

PR 5 *Arrange the improvisation environment with attention to the relative positioning of the instruments, the players, and the leader.*

Once the instruments have been selected for the experience, the next decision involves how to arrange the surroundings, either before the group arrives or before the improvisation experience begins. As Bruscia (1987) notes, "The arrangement of the room determines what kinds of interactions and relationships are apt to develop between the client, therapist, and media (e.g., instruments)" (p. 526). When possible, it is recommended that group members and the therapist sit in chairs or wheelchairs in a circle with the instruments placed in the center of the circle on the floor (or on a table if appropriate). Children who are too small for chairs can be positioned in a circle on the floor. In this case the therapist may either be in a low chair or on the floor, depending upon the needs of the group. (Note: When my students work with groups on the floor, they need to be reminded to position themselves on their bent knees and toes; this pose allows them freedom and swiftness of movement that they would not have while seated cross-legged on the floor.) A circle configuration allows for each person to be seen and heard and communicates equality of membership. It may become important to suggest that players change their position in the circle from time to time, in that sitting in a different place may affect what is seen and heard and the types of relationships that develop within the group. In fact, one technique for reenergizing a group or combating boredom or distraction is to ask the group members to reposition themselves prior to starting a new improvisation.

As with the selection of instruments, their arrangement deserves careful consideration. It makes good sense to place the large instruments such as the djembe, bongos on a stand, gong, etc., between the chairs so that they do not block the clients' visibility. Each instrument arranged on the floor ought to be set apart from its neighbor, and necessary accoutrements (mallets and strikers) placed immediately beside or on top of each instrument so that it is evident that they belong together. I have encountered therapists who place an instrument under each chair before the players enter the room, regardless of the clients' needs or clinical objectives. Most players do not notice the instruments, and they select their seats—and hence, their instruments—at random. While this type of arrangement might provide a structure necessary for certain players or certain clinical aims, it also negates free choice and may inhibit expression.

Of course, there will always be exceptions to the recommended arrangement. For example, therapists improvise in cramped hospital rooms with patients and their families; here it may be virtually impossible to position the group in a circle with the instruments in the center. Likewise, with large groups (camps, workshops, assemblies) this configuration may not work. Moreover, when therapists work with groups of children who have behavior disorders or who are highly impulsive, it may be contraindicated to display an entire array of instruments at once. Be sure to consider, also, that certain alternative configurations may actually promote certain aims. For example, if the goal is to help clients form more intimate relationships within the larger group, players may be asked to share a drum with rotating partners while seated face to face, or to make musical connections with others while moving about the room with their instruments.

Ex 3–8 (Experiential Learning)

Imagine you use improvisation throughout the workday with a variety of groups ranging in size from 4 to 12 members. Practice arranging and rearranging the room, chairs, and instruments for an effective experience.

PRESENTING THE INSTRUMENTS

Competencies addressed in this section include the ability to:

PR 6   *Present/Introduce the instruments to the players in a manner that enables their effective use.*

The final preparatory competency in this chapter refers to the presentation of the instruments that you have selected and arranged. Too often, music therapists assume that their clients will know how to sound their instrument or that they will be able to figure it out on their own. While this may be the case for some, it does not hold true for all players.

Murow (2002) writes:

> For the clients the first contact with music therapy is to discover
> the instruments (mainly percussion instruments), the way they
> sound, and the different ways they can be played. For most of
> them that is the first time they had been in contact with this kind
> of musical instruments. At the beginning, some clients have a
> hard time understanding what music therapy is; some think they
> are going to get music lessons and get frustrated when they
> realize they are not going to get lessons and they ask "how they
> are going to get better playing and singing?" As in any
> therapeutic process, clients have to learn how to use the medium,
> and when they learn about all the possibilities the music
> experience offers they become involved in the process!

Typically, there is cause to expedite the client's acquisition of
knowledge and skill so that the therapeutic work can be more purposeful
and accomplished more readily. If you are working in a short-term care
facility, for instance, you may improvise with a particular client only two
or three times; the work that you do together must proceed without
hesitation. Therefore, it is crucial that the therapist present some form of
introduction to the instruments prior to improvising, especially with (1)
the use of ethnic or novel instruments with which the clients may be
unfamiliar, (2) new group members, (3) groups in which members have
memory difficulties, and (4) groups in which members experience
anxiety or feel intimidated by the presence of musical instruments upon
which they are expected to "perform." Loth (in Davies & Richards, 2002)
writes about the importance of introducing the instruments to clients with
eating disorders prior to improvising:

> Before a patient joins the group, therefore, I take her into the
> music room and explain what happens in the group and what
> music therapy is about. ... I then encourage her to try out all the
> instruments, explaining the range of sounds available and the
> potential musical 'vocabulary.' This does something to lessen
> the potency of her fear in the group so that she does not have to
> act entirely from a position of defence, but can allow herself to
> engage with the group a little. The situation is analogous to a

mother bringing a child into a family meal in which a huge array of new and exotic food is presented. ... By taking her alone into the dining room beforehand and encouraging her to have a little taste of everything first, she can come to the table with a little more confidence in her ability to join the meal. (pp. 96–97)

Sound Vocabulary

A helpful introductory procedure is called the *Sound Vocabulary*. The sound vocabulary consists of a six-step procedure, modified in response to existing client knowledge and skill, depth of knowledge and skill required for success in the experience, and allotted time:

1. Pick up an instrument and announce what it is called ("This is a bodhran").

2. Share a bit of information about the instrument's origin, history, or conventional role ("This is an Irish drum, typically played in small Celtic folk bands along with pennywhistles and fiddles").

3. Demonstrate or describe the conventional way to sound the instrument, if known ("This instrument is typically played in a rapid fashion with a small, two-sided wooden beater").

4. Demonstrate at least two unconventional ways to sound the instrument ("One can play on the head with the palm of the hand or scratch the surface with the tips of the fingers").

5. Ask for volunteers or pass the instrument around the group for further demonstrations of how to sound the instrument.

6. Once all of the instruments have been introduced, instruct the clients to spend a few moments sounding and exploring each of the instruments. (All players do this simultaneously, unless there are contraindications.)

7.   After the exploration phase, and depending upon the type of improvisation to ensue, you may want to invite the clients to return to their chairs with an instrument(s) of their choice.

When presenting the sound vocabulary, try to adhere to the following guidelines:

- Use language that the clients can understand.

- Stress that authentic self-expression is of the highest order of playing, and that a perceived lack of musical knowledge and skill or experience with improvisation need not prevent this.

- When modeling how to sound the instruments, use both rhythmic and nonrhythmic examples.

- Incorporate a variety of dynamics, timbres, and playing configurations into your playing so that the clients can hear and see the various possibilities.

- Avoid putting emotional labels on certain sounds ("You can make a *sad* sound like this") and judging the value of certain sounds ("You might get a *better* sound if you play like this").

- When demonstrating the instruments, be careful not to play in such a sophisticated or showy manner that the clients are intimidated or apprehensive about their own performance skill.

- Consider the attributes of the players. Children need fewer words and more modeling; older adults may require a slower pace, etc.

Ex 3–9 (Experiential Learning)

Present a sound vocabulary to a group of 5 to 7 players. Practice with three different time parameters: 1 minute, 3 minutes, and 5 minutes. Practice as if presenting to children, adolescents/adults, and older adults.

Now that you have explored the terms and instruments of improvisation, it is time to consider the musical elements that are employed when therapists and clients improvise. This is the subject of the next chapter.

Vocabulary for Chapter Three

1.   *Instrumentarium*
2.   *Matched Grip*
3.   *Traditional Grip*
4.   *Ambidexterity*
5.   *Strikers*
6.   *Shakers*
7.   *Scrapers*
8.   *Motor Functioning*
9.   *Strength/Endurance*
10. *Coordination/Dexterity*
11. *Sound Variability*
12. *Expressive Potential*
13. *Sound Vocabulary*

Chapter Four

MUSICAL ELEMENTS OF IMPROVISATION

All music is composed of elements, fundamental "building blocks" that we stack together in various configurations to produce unique sounds. In this chapter, I will identify and define the rhythmic, tonal, textural, dynamic, and timbral elements that we characteristically use in clinical music improvisation. Information about the elements will assist us as we continue with subsequent skill-building exercises, and specifically as we encounter the Improvisation Assessment Profiles in Chapter Eight. Within each of the sections on rhythmic, tonal, textural, dynamic, and timbral elements below, exercises are included to help you solidify your perception and understanding of these concepts and begin to gain competency in employing them. As asserted above, the ability to manipulate the musical elements in an intentional way is absolutely critical to your success as a facilitator of clinical improvisation.

RHYTHMIC ELEMENTS

Competencies addressed in this section include the ability to:

PR 7   *Identify the rhythmic elements commonly used in clinical improvisation.*
PR 8   *Establish and maintain pulse in a variety of tempi.*
PR 9   *Establish and maintain subdivisions of the pulse.*
PR 10   *Establish duple and triple meters with the use of dynamic accents.*
PR 11   *Create simple and complex rhythmic patterns in duple and triple meters.*
PR 12   *Create effective rhythmic flourishes.*

The rhythmic elements used in clinical improvisation are pulse, tempo, subdivision, meter, rhythmic figure, and rhythmic flourish. All rhythmic elements have to do with the organization of sound duration—in other words, the long and the short of it!

Without exception, rhythmic playing begins with a *pulse*— sometimes called the *basic beat*, and this element either is made manifest (sounded) or remains latent (unsounded yet internal and "understood"). Like your heartbeat, musical pulse is a series of sounds that mark off time into "equal, recurring segments" (Bruscia, 1987, p. 465). It is steady, predictable, and static. The word "static" here implies stability and sameness (much like a "static referent" was previously described). When an individual is maintaining or listening to the musical pulse, there is no sense of urgency or forward drive; rather, there is a state of equilibrium. You can liken this to the way you feel when your heart is beating at a comfortable resting rate. The pulse, or basic beat, as we shall see in subsequent chapters, can serve as an important clinical grounding tool, providing a sense of comfort and stability for clients and therapists.

Just as your heart beats at various speeds, so too does the musical pulse occur at different rates. The rate of the pulse, that is, how frequently the sound evenly punctuates a given period of time, is called the *tempo*. In fact, the word "tempo" means "time." Tempo can change in one of three directions; quite obviously, the music can speed up *(accelerando),* slow down *(ritardando),* or ebb and flow *(rubato).*

Tempo is one representation of the energy, force, and motivation with which a player produces music. With an increase in the tempo comes a greater level of playing and listening activity, and we experience an accompanying boost in energy; likewise, when the tempo decreases, less activity is implied, and we feel the energy level diminish. This connection has clinical significance as we both assess and attempt to help group members alter their physical or psychological energy levels.

You are undoubtedly familiar with the many traditional Italian terms that we use to describe tempo, such as "lento," "moderato," "presto," and so on. In this book, I will use just five gradations, represented by the following terms: very slow, slow, moderate, fast, and very fast. I do this because these terms are more "client-friendly" than the Italian words.

Ex 4–1 (Experiential Learning)

As a group, place and feel the pulse somewhere on your body (legs, hands, chest, etc.). Without stopping, beat in an unaccented manner for several minutes as you work your way from very slow to very fast and back again. How was your energy level and attention affected as you moved through the continua of tempi?

Ex 4–2 (Experiential Learning)

As a group, place and feel the pulse somewhere on your body (legs, hands, chest, etc.) or on an instrument. Establish a common pulse in a moderate tempo; alternate playing this for 8 beats and internalizing the beat for 8 beats (hear and feel it but do not play it out loud). Extend the internalized beat to 16 beats or more. Is every player's concept of the tempo identical?

When the pulse is subdivided, it simply means that where time was evenly punctuated by one sound unit, now it is equally divided by more than one: two, three, four, and so on. As with tempo, *subdivisions* serve to add to the energy surrounding the pulse. With the increase in physical energy required to move from playing the pulse to playing subdivisions, there is an accompanying increase in and accumulation of auditory and perceptual energy.

Ex 4–3 (Experiential Learning)

Somewhere on your body (legs, hands, chest, etc.) or on an instrument, play and feel the pulse for 16 beats. Without stopping, double the pulse for 16 beats (duple subdivisions). Now double it again (quadruple). Repeat the cycle, beginning with the pulse. Concentrate on how it feels and sounds to subdivide the pulse in this manner. Repeat the exercise, subdividing in groups of three (triple) and six (sextuple).

One way of organizing a basic beat or its subdivisions is to use *meter*. Musical meter refers to the grouping of the pulse into numerical units. In duple meter, the pulse is grouped in twos and manifested as one emphasized or "strong" beat followed by one deemphasized or "weak" beat (or derivatives and combinations of this configuration). In triple meter, the pulse is grouped in threes and manifested as one strong beat followed by two weak beats (or derivatives and combinations of this configuration). Such organization creates a hierarchy of energy and time, which can help to order and contain rhythmic expressions. Metric groupings can be accomplished in a number of ways; in instrumental improvisation, the most common way to create strong and weak beats and thus create meter is through the use of dynamic accents.

Ex–4 (Experiential Learning)

Using your body (legs, hands, chest, etc.) or an instrument, practice playing and feeling the pulse in groupings of two (duple), three (triple), and four (duple extended), with dynamic accents on beat 1. Be sure to exaggerate the dynamic contrasts between accented and nonaccented beats. Which metric system, duple or triple, feels more comfortable to you as you use it?

Now we come to *rhythmic figure*, sometimes called *rhythmic pattern*. Players create figures or patterns by employing sounds that vary in length, emphasis, and alignment with each other or with the underlying pulse. Rhythmic figures range in complexity from combinations of simple subdivisions of the basic beat, to those that are based upon syncopation (emphasized sounds that do not align with the basic beat or metric structure), frequent subdivision changes (doubling to tripling or vice versa), or cross-rhythms (rhythmic patterns that fall outside the established metric structure). Rhythmic patterns lend interest and vitality to improvisation and quite obviously demand a higher level of organizational skill than pulse or subdivision.

Language and Rhythm

Some individuals are more adept at forming spontaneous rhythmic patterns than others, yet each of us can use our knowledge of and comfort with rhythmicity in language as one way to begin creating unique patterns and phrases. (The Orff-Schulwerk and Suzuki methods of music education are heavily dependent upon this fundamental connection between language and rhythm.) You have probably noticed that there is a certain inherent *prosody,* or pattern of intonation, to the words, phrases, and sentences that you speak on a daily basis. For example, the name "Cynthia Mallory Margaret Callahan" might suggest two measures of eighth notes in 6/8 meter. A phrase such as "Let's go down to the park!" on the other hand, might suggest 4/4 meter, with two eighth notes ("Let's go"), a quarter-note triplet or an eighth note followed by two sixteenth notes ("down to the"), and a quarter note ("park") followed by a quarter rest. You can create language-based rhythmic patterns and phrases using a wide range of text media, such as the players' names, everyday conversational phrases, and even published metric poetry.

Ex 4–5 (Experiential Learning)

As a group, and then individually within the group, practice saying and subsequently playing various words, phrases, and complete sentences. Use slight dynamic accents to indicate stressed syllables in the text.

Ex 4–6 (Experiential Learning)

One way to understand how figures are organized into coherent phrases is to play the melodic rhythms of pre-existing songs. Be sure to use material from a variety of genres, since different styles of music suggest different rhythmic configurations. Case in point: Compare the melodic rhythms of (1) "Twinkle Twinkle," a children's song composed of six identical rhythmic phrases consisting of even subdivisions, (2) "The Girl from Ipanema," a bossa nova with extensive syncopation, and (3) "The Star Spangled Banner," a patriotic song with many dotted note configurations.

Ex 4–7 (Experiential Learning)

As an ensemble, establish a moderate pulse somewhere on your body (feet, hands, chest, etc.) or on an instrument. Add an accent on the first of every 4 beats to create distinct measures of duple meter. Play four measures (16 beats) of pulse and four measures (16 beats) of improvised rhythmic figures; repeat. Experiment with simple subdivisions, syncopated rhythms, and cross-rhythms. Try to watch and listen for other players' rhythms while you play.

Variation: Sometimes I play the chord progression for the chorus to "Hit the Road, Jack" on the piano as a structure for this exercise. The players sing the chorus together and maintain the pulse (16 beats), and then I continue the harmonic progression while they improvise rhythmic figures (16 beats). I have found this to be a good way to encourage the use of swing-style rhythms, which do not seem to naturally appear in neophyte improvisations.

Although we can think of a *rhythmic flourish* as a subset of a rhythmic pattern, it has disparate qualities and can function differently from a pattern. Here, I define a flourish as a sudden or sporadic, brief, ornamental musical statement that serves to embellish the ongoing rhythmic sequences of an improvisation. Thus, by definition, rhythmic flourishes appear once in a while rather than consistently, are somewhat showy in that they are more sophisticated than the underlying rhythmic patterns, and, when used most effectively, function to lend beauty or interest to the improvisation. In clinical improvisation, a flourish can also be used to draw attention to some aspect of the music or to the player who introduces it. Flourishes are akin to what drum set players call "fills"—a pinch of salt or pepper to add a bit of flavor.

Let us take a moment to discuss the inherent *figure-ground* associations that exist between the rhythmic elements. The term figure-ground refers to the forefront-background relationships that comprise our ongoing perceptual fields—in this case, our auditory/perceptual field. It should be obvious that the pulse is always a ground and never a figure. Subdivisions played "against" or "on top of" a pulse could be considered a figure "against" or "on top of" a ground, but the line of distinction here is fuzzy. Certainly, when subdivisions are first introduced, they sound different from pulse and stand out, implying energy and movement toward some kind of musical activity or event; however, when they are repeated and then maintained, subdivisions begin to function as a ground. Rhythmic patterns, with their varied sound durations, emerge as foreground or figure against the ground, which could be the pulse (manifest or latent), its subdivisions, or a meter. Rhythms stand out not only because they are different from the ground, but also because they are typically non cyclical. Here, as with subdivisions, however, if a rhythmic pattern is repeated without change, it too may begin to function as a rhythmic ground. We might call this a *rhythmic ostinato*, by definition, a repeating and persistent rhythmic pattern; in fact, the word *ostinato* means "obstinate," or "unrelenting." Finally, a rhythmic flourish could be considered a figure against the rhythmic figure it is intended to embellish as well as against the underlying meter and pulse.

You may know from your own performance experiences that *rubato* playing within a group is often conducted. The word rubato means "robbed," a reference to the long notes stealing time from the short. Tempo is disregarded, but not so much so that the perception of rhythm is completely destroyed. In the strictest sense, then, rubato is a concept that applies to pulsed rather than unpulsed improvisation. Because rubato is such a powerful expressive tool, I believe it can be a useful tool in clinical improvisation.

Exercise 4–8 (Experiential Learning)

Use binary form (AB) to explore the contrast between rhythmic and rubato playing. The A section will be composed of group rhythmic playing; the B section will be solo rubato playing. Predetermine the length of each A section, but allow the soloist in the B section to cue the return to A. What was this like?

As a facilitator, it will be important that you are intentional about the types of rhythmic expressions you make. Serving as a rhythmic ground for other players is certainly a much different endeavor than that of playing varied rhythmic figures or adding occasional embellishments. Clinical outcomes may differ, depending upon the "rhythmic role" you assume in a group improvisation. The ability to select, manifest, and fluidly move between these roles must be developed. This final rhythmic exercise is designed to heighten awareness of rhythmic roles and provide opportunities to shift between roles in a responsive manner.

Ex 4–9 (Experiential Learning)

While improvising in a small group with body sounds or instruments, make conscious and ongoing decisions about your rhythmic role. Choose to (1) serve as a rhythmic ground by providing the pulse or fashioning a simple rhythmic ostinato, (2) play varied rhythmic figures above the pulse, (3) add rhythmic flourishes, or (4) listen carefully to the other members' rhythmic contributions. Assume the role that you perceive is most needed at any given time. Afterwards, discuss the roles you played.

Which roles were most comfortable for you? Least comfortable? What did you learn?

TONAL ELEMENTS

Competencies addressed in this section include the ability to:

PR 13 Identify the tonal elements commonly used in clinical *improvisation.*

PR 14 *Create melodies in a variety of modalities and tonalities.*

PR 15 *Improvise simple harmonic structures.*

PR 16 *Memorize and reproduce several harmonic vamps.*

The tonal features of improvisation are melody, modality, tonality, and harmony, and all of these are based upon the concept of pitch, which refers to the height or depth of a tone relative to other tones. Pitches are combined in particular sequences to form *melodies* of varying lengths and contours. Ordinarily melodies derive from and are embedded in *scales*, which are a series of adjacent pitches arranged in vertical fashion from low to high or vice versa (the Latin word "scala" means "ladder.") By definition, each unique scale or *modality* offers specific tones and intervals that can be used as fodder for the creation of melody. Not only do the tones of a melody have a specific highness or lowness and relationship to one another, but they also have a given duration, and it is the combination of the organization of pitch and rhythm that gives each melody its characteristic sound.

Scales and the melodies that derive from them are situated around a "home tone" or "tonic." The tonic is the tone to which all other tones in the scale or melody lead, aurally, and at which point there is a sense of rest or resolution. The *tonality* of a given scale is defined by (and named after) this resting tone. For example, a scale based on the white keys of the piano and starting on C (C-D-E-F-G-A-B-C) would claim C as its resting tone and thus its tonality.

Take a look at Table 6 below. This table contains a collection of scales and modes that share a D tonality. (D is used as the resting tone because the pitches that comprise the scales/modes in this tonality fall within the range of pitches found on most chromatic bell sets, which I use frequently for practice in the improvisation course.) Notice that each scale is made up of a sequence of unique pitches and, thus, distinctive intervals. With the exception of the chromatic, blues, and whole tone scales, if the interval between the resting tone and the third pitch of the sequence is a major third (4 semi-tones), the scale/mode is considered to have a major quality. If the same interval is a minor third (3 semi-tones), the scale/mode is considered to have a minor quality. You will need this table for the following exercise, and I believe it will be useful as you engage in further melodic improvisations. (Note: Another helpful resource is *Exploring Jazz: Scales for Keyboard* by Bill Boyd, Hal Leonard Publishing Corporation. Major and minor pentatonic and blues scales, progressions, and playing exercises comprise this manual.)

Table 6
Scales/Modes Built on D

Chromatic	D	D#	E	F	F#	G	G#	A	A#	B	C	C#	D▲
	D	Eb	E	F	Gb	G	Ab	A	Bb	B	C	Db	D▼
Dorian	D		E	F		G		A		B	C		D
Natural Minor	D		E	F		G		A	Bb		C		D
Harmonic Minor	D		E	F		G		A	Bb			C#	D
Melodic Minor	D		E	F		G		A		B		C#	D ▲
	D		E	F		G		A	Bb		C		D ▼
Major	D		E		F#	G		A		B		C#	D
Mixolydian	D		E		F#	G		A		B	C		D
Gypsy	D	Eb			F#	G		A	Bb			C#	D
Chinese Pentatonic (1)	D		E		F#			A		B			(D)
Chinese Pentatonic (2)	D		E			G		A		B			(D)
Japanese Pentatonic	D	Eb				G		A	Bb				(D)

Blues (Minor)	D			F		G	G#	A			C		D
Blues (Major)	D		E	F	F#			A		B			D
Whole Tone	D		E		F#		G#		A#		C B#		D

Ex 4–10 (Experiential Learning)

As a group and using chromatic bell sets (or another chromatic instrument), play each scale/mode in Table 6 in ascending and descending fashion several times. Use a variety of tempi, from very slow to very fast. Decide whether the scale is essentially major or minor. What words or images can you use to depict the characteristic sound or mood of each scale/mode? Does tempo affect the character? If so, how?

Pitches are not only combined sequentially, but they are combined vertically into *harmony* as well. When related pitches are sounded together, we call them *chords*. A sequence of chords is referred to as a harmonic *progression, chord changes,* or, simply, *changes*. In Appendix D, you will find several harmonic progressions that, when repeated, serve as useful structures for sustained melodic improvisation. Sometimes we call a repetitive harmonic pattern a *vamp*.

Now, let us revisit the concept of figure-ground as it applies to tonal elements. Just as a pulse serves as a ground for subdivisions and rhythmic figures, the scale or modality serves as a ground for melody. As such, we can say that the melody is a figure in relationship to a ground. If a melodic sequence is created solely from the notes of a given scale (C major), we can say that it is grounded in the modality. If it has the same resting tone as that scale (C), we can say that it is grounded in the tonality as well. Because harmony is also formed from pitches within a scale, it too can be considered a figure in relationship to this ground; however, in improvisation, harmony often serves as a ground for juxtaposed melodies or melodic fragments, akin to how a rhythmic ostinato (composed of subdivisions of the beat) serves as a ground for more discrete rhythmic figures.

Perhaps it is obvious that a melody can be grounded in a given modality but not share the tonality of an underlying scale. For example, assume that two people are improvising together. The first player is playing a repetitive C major chord (C,E, and G), thereby establishing a major modality and a C tonality. The other player is improvising a melodic sequence (C-G-E-D-C-B-C). This sequence is grounded in the modality and tonality of the harmony. However, when the second player shifts to another sequence (A-E-C-D-E-E-A) above the continuing C major chord of the first, the two improvisers no longer share a tonal ground even though they are playing from the same group of pitches.

Ex 4–11 (Independent Skill Development)

You will need to work in pairs over multiple sessions to complete this exercise. One player will provide harmonic support in the form of rhythmic ostinati and nonpulsed patterns, and using compatible pitches (e.g., D and A) on bass tone bars or the low range of the piano. The other player will create melodic figures over the ground within each of the scales/modes in Table 6. Use a chromatic bell set (with two mallets) or any other melodic instrument with the necessary pitches. Audio-record the improvisations, play back, and discuss. In which of the scales/modes was it easiest to improvise? Most difficult? Which specific features did you like about the pieces you created together?

Ex 4–12 (Independent Skill Development)

Memorize several of the vamps that appear in Appendix D. With a different partner, practice improvising melodies with each of the vamps. Which ones do you find most useful, and why?

TEXTURAL ELEMENTS

Competencies addressed in this section include the ability to:

PR 17 Identify the textural elements commonly used in clinical improvisation.
PR 18 Assume a variety of musical roles to create a variety of textures.
PR 19 Demonstrate multiple playing configurations on each instrument.

In clinical improvisation, several aspects of texture emerge as important. In general, texture refers to "the overall fabric of the improvisation" (Bruscia, 1987, p. 406), a weaving that may involve various pitch registers, musical roles, and playing configurations.

Pitch register applies to tonal improvisation, and refers to the range of pitches used and changes therein. A related concept, *tessitura*, refers to the general highness or lowness of a part; unlike pitch register, tessitura can apply to nonpitched instruments. While most percussion instruments are nonpitched in the classic sense, they do have a highness or lowness about them and, when used together, suggest a pitch range. One could say that a large ngoma drum has a lower tessitura than a frame drum. There are, of course, certain "pitched" (yet nonmelodic) percussion instruments: agogo bells, bongos, chime tree, slit drum, talking drum, temple blocks, and triangle, to name a few.

Ex 4–13 (Experiential Learning)

As an extreme example of pitch register and tessitura, construct a three-section group improvisation. Play the first section on instruments with a high register (soprano glockenspiel, finger cymbals, piano upper register, claves, small drums, etc.); play the second section on instruments with a low register (bass tone bars, piano lower register, large drums, etc.); and play the final section on instruments from both registers. Contrast the sections. What differences did you hear? What sensations, thoughts, or emotions are triggered?

Musical roles relate to the various parts and how they function within the overall texture of the piece, that is, how they determine part-whole relationships. This aspect of texture applies to both rhythmic and tonal improvisation. A single line of music may serve as (1) a figure or a ground (as previously mentioned), as in a solo vocal line with piano accompaniment, (2) one of many equal parts sounding simultaneously, as in homophonic or polyphonic drumming, and (3) a leader or a follower, as in a dyadic improvisation in which one xylophone leads another. Sometimes these role relationships are unvarying throughout a single improvisation, and sometimes they change. In fact, if you hear a shift in the texture of the music, it most likely signals a change in role functions.

Note that the concept of musical roles is relevant to both group and solo improvisation. By definition, group improvisation is homophonic or polyphonic in nature. Most individual clients you will encounter in clinical improvisation are capable of producing monophonic sounds, with or without assistance. Clients with functional use of two limbs (two arms/hands or an arm and a leg) or with excellent dexterity in one hand are capable of playing homophonically or polyphonically. I once worked with a young man who, with the left side of his body paralyzed due to a head trauma, was able to produce three simultaneous musical lines by employing two mallets with his right hand and playing a tambourine with his foot! In fact, it was his self-determined challenge to create multiple voices, perhaps as a way to make up for the fact that a tracheotomy had left him without the use of his original voice.

Ex 4–14 (Experiential Learning)

As a group, experiment with each of the three musical role relationships specified above: (1) solo with accompaniment, (2) homophony or polyphony, in which each part has equal importance, and (3) leader and follower relationships. Talk about how each role within each of the three configurations places distinctive demands on the improvisers.

Texture is partially determined by *playing configurations*. Various configurations that result in specific textural "complexions" are a melody divided between two simultaneous parts (as in a passage of repeated intervals of a third or sixth), block chords or broken chords (as in a piano accompaniment), repeated notes and tremolos (as in a rapid alternation between the left and right hands on a drum), and *glissandi* (as in a sliding of the mallet up or down the bars of a metallophone). Without a doubt, there is a direct relationship between texture (playing configuration) and timbre; oftentimes a change in the playing configuration creates a distinct change in timbre, such as the difference between striking the head of a tambourine and simply shaking the jingles. However, there are also times when the playing configuration (and hence, the texture) changes but the timbre remains constant. Consider, for instance, three different ways of approaching a conga drum: (1) a series of single strikes in the center of the head, (2) a series of double strikes (two hands simultaneously) in the center of the head, and (3) a sustained roll (a rapid succession of *L-R* strikes) in the center of the head. All three result in the same timbre. However, the texture—the thinness or thickness of the sound, if you will—is quite obviously modified from one to the other. The first strike is clearly monophonic: one hand, one voice. The second strike is clearly homophonic: two hands, two voices. It sounds thicker than the first. The third is monophonic. In actuality, only one voice is sounding at a time, but depending upon the rapidity with which the hands alternate, there may be the aural illusion of thickness of texture.

Imagine the numerous textural possibilities and combinations that could emerge from a group consisting of one therapist and just three players: At any given time, one or more improvisers could be playing monophonically, homophonically, or polyphonically (on one or more instruments), playing a ground or a figure, creating a solo or providing an accompaniment, acting as a leader or following another player's lead, and exploring a variety of playing configurations. The concept of texture is multifaceted to begin with; when multiple players are involved, the challenges for the therapist as observer and facilitator seem to increase exponentially.

Ex 4–15 (Independent Skill Development)

Using a barred instrument (xylophone, metallophone, etc.) and two mallets, construct a 2-minute improvisation that incorporates all of the following playing configurations: single sequential pitches, thirds, sixths, three-note chords (this may be difficult), arpeggios, repeated pitches, tremolos (two different pitches), and glissandi. Audio-record your improvisation and play it for the entire group. Discuss the challenges and the outcome.

Ex 4–16 (Independent Skill Development)

Using a freestanding drum on which you can use both hands, construct an improvisation that incorporates all of the following playing configurations: single sequential strikes, double strikes (two hands at once), tremolos, and solo/accompaniment, in which one hand plays the pulse or a rhythmic ostinato and the other plays rhythmic figures. Audio-record your improvisation and play it for the entire group. Discuss the challenges and the outcome.

DYNAMIC ELEMENTS

Competencies addressed in this section include the ability to:

PR 20 *Identify the dynamic elements commonly used in clinical improvisation.*
PR 21 *Create gradual and sudden changes in volume.*

Dynamic elements are those elements relating to the mass and intensity of sound, or what we commonly refer to as *volume*. Like tempo, volume exists on a continuum, from sounds that are so soft they are barely audible, to sounds that are so loud they create pain or discomfort in the listener. In percussion-based clinical improvisation, because we often use acoustic instruments that are designed for one player each, we rarely encounter sounds that are so intense that they cause pain. However, I have noticed that prolonged or distinctive sounds (e.g., cabasa, ocean drum, shakeré, etc.), particularly at a high volume level, can create discomfort and anxiety. In instrumental improvisation, the relative intensity of sound results from the relative force applied to or through the sounding surface of the instrument used. So, the more force you apply to the head of a drum, for example, the louder that drum will sound, in general. With group improvisation, multiple instruments are sounding at once, which creates an additive effect.

Volume levels can stay the same or they can change. There are essentially two types of change: (1) abrupt modifications, as with a *piano subito* following a *forte* passage or the use of metered and unmetered dynamic accents and (2) gradual modifications, as with a *crescendo* or *decrescendo*. Unmetered accents are sometimes employed to lend vitality and interest to a rhythmic ground consisting of basic pulse (Wigram, 2004). Such accents can also be used to call attention to the person playing them, in that they are typically an unexpected departure from the steadiness of the dynamic level of the music. Therefore, if a therapist or client desires to be noticed, she or he might insert random accents into the music. A further use of unmetered accents is to add tension or throw the music "off kilter." This might be of value during an improvisation in which the players need a catalyst in order to take necessary risks in their improvising, or need to be re-engaged in the music after a period of interpersonal or intermusical isolation, inattention, or boredom. I caution the therapist against the overuse of random dynamic accents. The unexpected and poignant nature of these accents may create unwanted anxiety or distract or bother individuals who have cognitive or sensory processing deficits, and could create an unwelcome impression that the therapist is unpredictable and therefore can not be trusted.

A gradual crescendo produced through the gathering and building of energy and sound often suggests growing excitement, fortitude, tension, apprehension, etc. (Think about Ravel's *Bolero*.) A gradual decrescendo, created through a decrease in energy and resulting sound, often suggests diminishing excitement, lessening of tension, weakness, serenity, etc. Dramatic changes in loudness, especially when unexpected as with random dynamic accents, can convey surprise, fragmentation, impulsivity, freedom, etc. Players often use changes in the dynamic levels of their improvising to create, accumulate, and release physical and emotional tension.

Ex 4–17 (Experiential Learning)

Singularly or as a group, experiment with gradual crescendi followed by gradual decrescendi. Talk about the sensations that accompany this type of dynamic change, as well as the sensorimotor demands placed upon you.

Ex 4–18 (Experiential Learning)

As a group, practice using volume as a way to accumulate and release tension. What are some of the ways you accomplished this?

TIMBRAL ELEMENTS

Competencies addressed in this section include the ability to:

PR 22   *Identify the timbral elements commonly used in clinical improvisation.*
PR 23   *Demonstrate multiple timbres on each instrument.*

Timbre, which in French means "bell" or "tone," refers here to the quality and color of a sound produced by an instrument (including the voice). The timbre of an instrument as it is conventionally sounded is what helps us characterize it and recognize it as unique among other instruments. Each instrument is capable of producing more than one timbre or multiple variations of a fundamental timbre, and this feature can be used to communicate something about the passage or piece being played. We often use words like "dark," "bright," "thick," "thin," "harsh," "dull," "focused," and "breathy" to describe aspects of timbre. Most of the instruments that we use in clinical improvisation have a wide range of timbral possibilities, because they can be sounded in so many different ways. For example, a headed tambourine can be shaken; struck with the open or fisted hand or other part of the body; struck with a wood, felt, or rubber mallet; and scratched with the fingertips. Each of these playing configurations results in the production of a unique timbre. Some instruments have more potential for variation than others; these are the instruments that we typically think of as inherently more expressive (see Chapter Three).

Ex 4–19 (Experiential Learning)

Explore timbre in a series of nonrhythmic, referential group improvisations. Use referents mentioned in the above section ("dark," "bright," etc.). Develop your own list of words to describe timbre and play these referents. Discuss.

Vocabulary for Chapter Four

1. *Musical elements*
2. *Pulse*
3. *Basic beat*
4. *Subdivisions*
5. *Meter*
6. *Rhythmic Figure*
7. *Rhythmic Pattern*
8. *Prosody*
9. *Rhythmic Flourish*
10. *Figure-Ground*

11. *Rhythmic Ostinato*
12. *Rubato*
13. *Melody*
14. *Modality*
15. *Tonality*
16. *Harmony*
17. *Harmonic Progression*
18. *Harmonic Changes*
19. *Vamp*
20. *Pitch Register*
21. *Tessitura*
22. *Musical Roles*
23. *Playing Configurations*
24. *Volume*
25. *Crescendo*
26. *Decrescendo*
27. *Timbre*

Chapter Five

STRUCTURES FOR IMPROVISATION

One common misconception about clinical improvisation is that there is no structure for the music-making experience, and as a consequence, that there is nothing for the therapist to plan ahead of time. In fact, this is rarely the case; various structures actually exist on at least three levels. First, there are structures of the overall process of improvisation-based therapy, which may involve multiple sessions. Structures at this macro level may be referred to as sequential *phases* of treatment. Examples include *developing rapport, identifying issues or themes for treatment, working through, and terminating.* At the next level, many therapists determine structures or formats for each improvisational session, such as that suggested by Stephens (1984): warm-up, verbal discussion, core experience, and closing. On the third level, each singular improvisational experience within the session typically has some kind of organizational structure, or parameter. Even in so-called "free" improvisation, in which no parameters are determined or imposed ahead of time, structures may and often do emerge as the music unfolds over time. In her writings on structure in Analytical Music Therapy, Priestley (1994) refers to the human tendency to impose structure on life activity where there is none readily offered:

> This reminds us of the strange fact that people faced with complete freedom from some past-imposed discipline usually proceed to write their own Book of Leviticus to give themselves the security of the structure, sense of direction and identity that they have lost. (p. 127)

Hadsell's (1993) notions about external structure are relevant here. She notes that three levels of structure—maximum, moderate, and minimum—can be applied differentially to the various environmental aspects of music therapy, including the "activity" (the improvisation experience). For example, a highly structured improvisation experience would involve therapist-sequenced events and task analysis. On the other hand, an improvisation experience with minimum structure would involve collaboration between the client and therapist in planning and flexibility to rearrange steps in the process. Hadsell writes:

> The type and amount of structure is client specific, environment specific, and task specific. If any of these aspects of a situation change, adjustments in structure may be required. External factors such as medication, family interactions, and previous day's events may alter the needed amount of structure. Therefore, the therapist must constantly monitor the stage of therapy in which the client is operating and respond to fluctuations in the client's need for structure even during a single music therapy session. (p. 63)

That stated, the focus of this chapter is the planful development or selection of structures for the improvisation session and experience.

SESSION STRUCTURES

Competencies addressed in this section include the ability to:

PR 24   Identify suitable structures for improvisation sessions.

In this section of the chapter, I will discuss some of the ways in which session structures are helpful to the process of therapy. We will then provide some sample session formats and give you an opportunity to develop your own. What do you think might be some of the benefits of employing session structures?

1. Structures lend predictability. Recall the discussion in Chapter Three about preparing the players to use the instruments. When clients know something about what to expect during an improvisation session and can predict certain aspects of their experience, they are less likely to feel confused. Consistency and predictability can ease the anxiety that often accompanies the prospect of risk and change. With reduced confusion and anxiety, clients are more likely to trust the therapist, the

other group members, and the process of improvisation. Increased trust can open the doors to clinical rapport.

2. <u>Structures lend logic.</u> When an improvisation session possesses some kind of structure, it tends to flow in a logical way. Events are perceived as sequential yet interrelated. Significant aspects of the clients' experiences are more effable and memorable when attached to an organizational framework.

3. <u>Structures lend equality and cohesion.</u> When many clients come together, there are bound to be multiple abilities, needs and clinical aims, personalities, and levels of maturity. While this degree of heterogeneity can add a richness to group dynamics, it can also contribute to a perception of inequality and fragmentation within the group. Without a session structure, musical and interpersonal interactions may be stilted and chaotic. However, when improvisers with divergent attributes proceed together through a structured session, they suddenly have a common focus. Players are equally valued in the process of music-making, and there is increased potential for the perception of "we-ness" to develop as the individuals rally around the challenges inherent in each sequential component of the session.

4. <u>Structures lend meaning.</u> In reflection, clients and therapists can comprehend the significance of their actions and experiences if they have a framework for doing so. Aigen (1998) writes about a five-stage session structure that became evident as he analyzed Paul Nordoff's improvisational sessions with an adolescent client. The structure, *opening-transition-working-transition-closure*, assisted Aigen in making sense of the nature of the client's experience and Nordoff's interventions. He states:

> In order to understand the significance of a clinical intervention, it is necessary to perceive it in relation to the stage of the session in which it occurs. This is one of the many contexts of meaning in which it becomes intelligible. There are different tasks associated with each stage of the session, and a given

intervention must be considered in relation to these tasks in order to understand its rationale. (p. 168)

As mentioned above, Stephens (1984) recommends a four-part group session structure in her model of improvisation, termed *Adult Improvisational Music Therapy*. I have used Stephens's sequence in my work with adults in short-term psychiatric settings, the population for which the format was developed. With some modifications, I find that this structure can be effective in other treatment settings and with adolescents and children as well.

The first component of Stephens's session structure is the *warm-up*, a free (nonreferential) improvisation, the purpose of which is to gather the group members and promote self-awareness. The second phase is the *verbal discussion*, during which clients share what has occurred since the last session and target issues and concerns for therapy. The *working through* is the third and main phase. During the working through, improvisation and discussion are used to explore the identified issues, generate solutions to problems and conflicts, release energy, and consolidate insights gained through the therapy process. At the end of each session, there is a period of *closure*, during which clients may improvise, sing, or quietly reflect as a way to acknowledge the work that has been accomplished.

Now, let us work through a case study to illustrate some of the decisions you must make in order to determine a suitable session structure for one particular group of adults. Be aware that this vignette is designed with verbal clients in mind and that verbal interventions may be used in tandem with music improvisation.

Vignette 5–1

Imagine that you are working in a psychiatric hospital with a group of six to nine adult patients with varied mental illnesses such as schizophrenia, affective disorders, and personality disorders. Perhaps these individuals are coming together from disparate living units within the hospital for their first music therapy session. With 50 minutes, and having determined that improvisation is a suitable method for these particular patients and these conditions, what kind of session structure will you implement? Here are some of the questions you may ask and the factors you may consider throughout your process of discernment:

1.   *Is it necessary that I begin the session with some discussion?* Absolutely! These clients do not know one another, and they do not know me. I will need to begin with a brief introduction so they can start to learn one another's names. It is likely that some of them have never improvised, and it is a certainty that they have never improvised with one another. I will need to talk a bit about improvisation—what it is and is not, what they can expect to experience, how it may assist them, etc. There is likely to be elevated anxiety related to the clients' diagnoses as well as to the novelty of the situation. There also may be a high degree of social tension as different ages, genders, races, ethnicities, sexual orientations, and personalities merge for the first time. I may need to reassure the clients with a brief discussion about expectations related to physical and psychological safety and confidentiality. It may even be necessary to establish some rules for our work together.

2.   *Will a verbal check-in be necessary?* Perhaps. A check-in typically includes a statement of how each person is feeling and what issues are on her or his mind at the time of the session. In ongoing therapy, a check-in may also include a recapitulation of events or actions since the last session. Since this is a fledgling group, it may be prudent to offer the clients the option to say something personal, while also offering the option to pass. In the future, an instrumental check-in might be helpful.

3.   *Shall I provide a sound vocabulary?* Of course! The instruments we will be using are unfamiliar to most of the clients. Naming and demonstrating each one will help them become more comfortable with the tools and language of improvisation. I will limit the number of instruments we use and the information that I share about each one so that I do not overwhelm the clients during this introductory phase.

4.   *Shall I plan a musical warm-up?* Yes! Once I have introduced the instruments, it may be important for the members of the group to begin playing immediately, especially if I sense that their anxiety is

mounting as time passes and, as a result, they are growing resistant. On the other hand, there may be excitement and enthusiasm once the instruments have been presented; I would like to capitalize on this.

5.   *Shall the warm-up involve group or solo playing?* Group playing! Because this is a first experience, and based on my assumption that there may be some initial anxiety, I think it is important to play as an ensemble. That way, individuals can "hide" within the music until they are ready to reveal something unique about themselves. When the clients are more confident with the instruments, their abilities, and their roles within the group, I will be able to introduce some solo playing.

6.   *Shall the warm-up be structured in any way?* Definitely! I believe it is critical that there be some predetermined and verbalized structure since this is our first improvisation experience together; in this case, structure may diminish confusion and anxiety. However, I do not want the warm-up to be so structured that the clients feel stifled in their expression, independence, or creativity. It is too early in the session and in their development as a group to expect that individuals would naturally connect with one another during the music-making, although I will watch and listen for this; however, the clients may be able to use the warm-up to develop some basic self-awareness of their physical and emotional states. Whatever givens I choose will be geared toward this aim.

7.   *Shall I choose instruments for the players?* No! I will let them select their own instruments because their choices and decision-making process could tell me something significant about them and their preferences. Additionally, allowing them to make their own choices validates their self-determinism and communicates that I trust them and respect their actions.

8.   *Shall we discuss the warm-up?* I don't know yet; I may have to decide this on the spot. Sometimes warm-ups are verbally processed, but often they are not. If, however, a client begins sharing in an unsolicited fashion and others join in productively, I certainly would not squelch that course of action! Some of the aspects of the warm-up that could come

forth are the clients' instrument choices, comfort, energy levels, sensory perceptions, emotional responses, and reactions to the musical product. I will be ready to facilitate some discussion on these topics, using active listening and verbal techniques.

9.   *What next, a core improvisation experience?* Yes! This is a juncture in the process during which I really need to remain open and flexible. Obviously, I want to move ahead with the clients' needs and clinical objectives in mind. These may be immediately apparent because they flow from the facility goals, assessment outcomes, or clients' treatment plans. Or, perhaps the needs and objectives will be evident during the warm-up, which can serve as a kind of in-the-moment assessment. Perhaps I will act upon a hunch. Finally, I may make a plan for the core experience based upon something that a client shares out loud. Whatever the case, and even if I have a predetermined plan, I need to be ready and feel free to respond to what is most salient at this particular point in time. One thing I know for sure is that all of the clients have been referred to this group because they need to practice interacting with others in positive and meaningful ways. Over time, I want this group to be a place where clients know they can "be themselves" with others, express difficult thoughts and feelings, and develop trust and empathy. With that in mind, the core experience will revolve around establishing preliminary connections with one another through musical interactions.

10.   *Shall I facilitate discussion about the core experience?* Yes! Here again, it is difficult to predict what will emerge as most important about the core improvisation, but in general, the verbal techniques I use (see Chapter Nine) will be designed to elicit patient verbalizations, focus the discussion around emerging issues, and validate authentic responses and meaningful insights.

11.   *Will we play again?* This will be entirely dependent upon factors such as time, client motivation, and what remains to be accomplished in the session, among other factors.

12. Is it necessary to have a distinct closing segment? Probably. With this group, it may be sufficient to close with a verbal summary of what has taken place during the session. However, if time permits and there is a valid reason to do so (again, if it meets a determined need or clinical objective), I would prefer to employ a musical closing, because all of the clients are involved in verbal psychotherapy several times each week, yet their opportunities for creative arts expression are severely limited. Further improvisation, singing, and brief reflective listening are reasonable options for musical closure.

So, having completed the above process, you have "fleshed out" the following session structure:

1. Introductory Discussion
2. Verbal Check-in (optional)
3. Sound Vocabulary
4. Warm-up Improvisation
5. Brief Discussion (optional)
6. Core Improvisation Experience
7. Verbal Processing
8. Verbal or Musical Closure

Ex 5–1 (Didactic Learning)

With a partner, select a clinical scenario from the list that appears below. Together, develop a session structure that seems well-suited to the attributes of the clients and the specified time frame. Share your session structure and your decision-making processes with other members of the group.

1. *Six elderly residents, mild dementia, 20-minute session.*
2. *Six school-aged children, specific learning disabilities, 30-minute session.*
3. *Six adolescents, severe behavior disorders, 45-minute session.*
4. *Six adults, various neurological impairments, 30-minute session.*

The next step in the planning process is to determine which structures, if any, may be applied to individual improvisations within the session. That brings us to the next section.

SELECTING AND PRESENTING GIVENS AND REFERENTS

Competencies addressed in this section include the ability to:

PR 25 Determine and present suitable givens and referents for improvisation experiences.

As defined in Chapter Two, a given can be considered a structure or parameter for improvisation, selected in response to one or multiple factors related to client need and/or clinical objective. Recall that the three categories of givens are vocabulary, procedural, and interpersonal. Vocabulary givens relate to the number or sorts of instruments and/or sounds that are used by the players, as in the following example:

> … Linda approached the piano, looking angry, and began to bang out loud tone clusters. When she agreed verbally that she was angry, the therapist asked her to try singing a song to express her anger verbally as well as physically (Dvorkin, 1998, p. 295).

Procedural givens often guide the sequence or length of an improvisation. Priestley (1994) writes:

> Another structure which is useful in dyadic improvisation is the limitation of a certain time span. I used to begin a certain patient's session with a 10-minute improvisation. We were quite free as far as subject matter was concerned and there were no musical constraints, but the realization that the time was limited made him pour his expression into the time available. (p. 132)

Interpersonal givens relate to relationships specified between the various improvisers, as in this excerpt:

As depression is often based on anger bound by guilt, I devised some exercises to express aggression in a non-threatening way on two 16-inch tom-toms. Each of them had to play on his own drum then reach over and bang on the other's drum. (Priestley, 1994, p. 287)

Selection

Further examples of all three types of givens appear in Appendix E. Take a look at No. 6 under *Vocabulary Givens*. This parameter refers to setting up the tonal instruments in a Chinese pentatonic scale. There are myriad possible factors that might steer a therapist (or the players) to select this particular given. The Chinese pentatonic scale, by virtue of its construction of whole steps, possesses little (if any) musical dissonance. All possible melodic and harmonic intervals in the scale are considered consonant intervals (major seconds and sixths, major and minor thirds, and perfect fourths and fifths). Because there are no semitones in this five-note scale, there is no tension-resolution cycle. My students often describe the Chinese pentatonic as "open," "unfinished," and "floaty," particularly when it is played in an unpulsed manner or in a moderate, slow, or very slow tempo. Now consider why a therapist (or the players) might want to avoid musical tension and build consonance and suspension into a group improvisation? Could it be that the group members are highly tense to begin with and need to experience a contrasting relief? Or maybe the therapist has limited the number of different pitches in the scale to five in order to make the instruments less complicated or intimidating. Or perhaps the scale is being used as a transition to an introspective music-assisted imagery experience. Each of these is a plausible explanation for the therapist's decision to select this particular vocabulary given.

Ex 5–2 (Didactic Learning)
Alone or with a partner, select two givens from each category presented in Appendix E. Working in reverse, so to speak, discern some factors that might have caused a therapist (or the players) to establish these givens and write these factors in the space provided. Be prepared to discuss your findings with the group.

Ex 5–3 (Didactic Learning)

Alone or with a partner, select a specific need and/or clinical objective and determine a vocabulary, procedural, or interpersonal given that might assist in addressing the need or objective. Be prepared to discuss your findings with the group .(Note: If desired, you may move from the group discussion immediately into the following exercise.)

As stated above, givens and referents may be selected during the session, as opposed to beforehand, on the basis of significant factors that emerge and deserve consideration. Here are a few:

1.   The energy level of the group as members enter the playing space (e.g., the players are physically active and talkative, which is a pleasant change; the therapist incorporates movement into the improvisation in order to sustain the desired level of energy).

2.   Casual comments that are made as members enter the playing space (e.g., a client says, "I really don't feel like being around anyone else today"; the therapist selects the referent, "leave me alone").

3.   Urgent stated or perceived emotional needs of (a) member(s) of the group (e.g., a member enters the room crying and talking about feeling like an abandoned child; the therapist invites her to sit in the center of the circle and asks the group members to improvise around her in a rocking fashion, softly and in 6/8 meter).

4.   An intuition of the therapist (e.g., the therapist feels a sense of intimacy developing between certain members of the group and asks them to improvise with one another in *dialogic,* or conversational, fashion and to subsequently talk about the experience).

5.   The request of an influential or trusted member of the group (e.g., a member who has assumed a parental or authoritative role in the group requests to use the drums as a way to release the anger that he senses is building up within the group).

6.   Modifications in the group configuration or facilitator(s) (e.g., several new individuals are unexpectedly referred to the group at once; the therapist asks veteran and new members to improvise in pairs).

7.   Unexpected modifications in the environment or the instrumentarium (e.g., due to a quarantine, the session is held on the unit rather than in the music therapy clinic, and the children are unable to use the instruments; the therapist suggests an improvisation using body sounds or objects in their environment).

8.   Modifications in the relationships between members of the group (e.g., two members are at odds with one another, and the tension between them is creating some division within the group; the therapist asks the dyad in question to share an instrument, improvise together, and subsequently discuss the experience).

9.   Needs and/or themes that emerge during a verbal check-in (e.g., during check-in, three members mention fear of alcohol relapse and one talks about fear of losing custody of a child; the therapist recommends an improvisation based upon the referent, "fear").

Keep in mind that there are, quite likely, infinite possibilities when it comes to the selection of givens for clinical improvisation. Treatment groups are made up of several clients, each a unique human being with a distinct personality and distinct needs. The therapist, as an authentic, communicative, flexible, and responsive leader (remember these terms?), can select and create givens that serve to provide for a meaningful and productive improvisation experiences. Staying open to the immediate needs of your clients will help you access your creative storehouse!

Presentation

The skills related to the verbal presentation of givens and referents are really no different from the skills necessary for other types of verbal interaction in the music therapy session. Here are a few reminders.

In general, it is recommended that the leader be as concise as possible when issuing or explaining givens and referents. The reason is simple: Long-winded directions and explanations can result in extreme boredom and/or confusion. I encourage leaders to say what needs to be said in four sentences or less, which is a formidable challenge at times. Further, it is always a good idea to check for (or, in young or nonverbal clients, watch for) comprehension—ask if the players have any questions about what has been said or what is expected of them.

One challenge is to match the vocabulary in the directions to the age and/or verbal abilities of the clients. For example, imagine that you are working with a group of clients with global developmental delays. If you were to say, "I will cue your entrances, so you need to focus your attention on me, please," the players would most likely stare at you blankly. They may have heard the words "cue" and "attention" but they may not understand their meanings. In this situation, it would be better to say simply, "Follow me!" When working with adolescents and adults who have typical verbal skills, I recommend that you use a vocabulary suited to a typical eighth-grader, which is the standard for most writing in the popular press. Certain musical terms, such as "timbre," "crescendo," "rondo form," "syncopation," etc., can be used freely once they have been defined within the group.

No matter how thoughtful the content of your instructions, your words may be lost on the players if the delivery is not solid. Aspects of pacing, volume, and pitch are of equal importance in the presentation of givens and referents for improvisation. Pacing is an issue with individuals who have difficulty processing spoken language due to neurological or sensory impairments. As a rule, I find that novice leaders tend to speak more quickly than they ought to when communicating with their players, often due to performance anxiety or a lack of clarity about what it is that they are trying to say.

Another common problem in beginning leaders is a tendency to speak too quietly with certain populations and too loudly with others. When the students at my university begin leading sessions in a local nursing care facility with elderly residents, most of whom have some hearing loss, the students must be constantly reminded to project their voices. A client's lack of comprehension due to her or his inability to hear the directions can be mistaken for a lack of interest or resistance— two responses that will swiftly undermine a novice leader's confidence, not to mention thwart therapy. On the other hand, it is not necessary to speak more loudly than usual to a person who has a visual impairment but adequate hearing.

If the therapist's voice is pitched exceptionally high, people with hearing loss in the upper register may have difficulty making sense of the directions. Also, a high-pitched voice may be appropriate when speaking to small children but may be perceived as condescending when used with adolescents, adults, and older adults. Finally, high-pitched voices may be associated with a lack of confidence, maturity, or authority.

Ex 5–4 (Experiential Learning)

Together, create a hypothetical client group of four to six members. Determine attributes of the group and at least one need or clinical objective. Determine several possible givens and select one or two to address attributes, needs, and/or objectives. Improvise and discuss the effectiveness of the given(s). Did it (they) match an attribute, fill a need, or fulfill an objective? How? If not, why not?

Ex 5–5 (Experiential Learning)

Conduct a brief verbal check-in with the group. From the information shared during this check-in, determine a referent that might meet one or more members' immediate needs. Play the referent and discuss the improvisation. Was the referent a good choice? Why or why not?

Vocabulary for Chapter Five

1.   *Phases*
2.   *Developing Rapport*
3.   *Identifying Issues*
4.   *Working Through*
5.   *Terminating*
6.   *Adult Improvisational Music Therapy*
7.   *Warm-up*
8.   *Verbal Discussion*
9.   *Core Experience*
10.   *Closure*
11.   *Verbal Check-in*
12.   *Dialogic Improvisation*

Chapter Six

NONMUSICAL FACILITATION SKILLS (VERBAL & GESTURAL)

The brief *verbalizations* and *gestures* of the therapist during the actual music-making are the focus of this chapter. As you will see, there are five identified competencies in this area, called *Nonmusical Facilitation*. Along with *Musical Facilitation* (Chapter Seven), these are the heart of the improvisational experience.

STARTING AND STOPPING

Competencies addressed in this section include the ability to:

NM 1 Start and stop the improvisation if necessary.

Once the instruments have been arranged, presented, and selected, and once relevant givens or referents have been established, it is time to start playing. Starting and stopping the music-making is the focus of the first competency.

Starting

Whose job is it to begin an improvisation? The answer to this question is, of course, "It depends." How a group begins playing depends upon several interdependent factors, some of which are age, need/clinical aim, previous improvisation experiences, and size of the group. There will be times when an improvisation begins freely and naturally, without any direction from the therapist. There will also be times when a group of players needs the guidance of the leader or the structure of a given to get off the ground. Let us explore several options for therapist intervention at this juncture of the process and the implications of each.

One highly structured way to begin an improvisation is to provide a *countdown* ("One, two, ready, play!"), just as a conductor might start a band, orchestra, or chorus. Consider the implications of this sort of guidance. It should be obvious that a countdown places a great deal of control in the hands of the person who is counting. When that individual counts, he or she may dictate tempo, meter, musical style, and even dynamic level. This type of authority may be necessary in certain situations, such as with highly anxious clients whose motor activity needs to be slowed. On the other hand, a countdown start can thwart free expression and independence and may be contraindicated with clients who have been controlled in the past through sexual, physical, and emotional abuse. Another, less directive, verbal cue is to say, "Let's play" or "Play with me." This type of cue signals that it is time to start without establishing the specifics of how that will occur.

A similar means of beginning is for the therapist or designated client simply to begin the playing without speaking. As with the countdown start, this affords the therapist (or client) an opportunity to set the general character of the improvisation—or at least the first few moments of the music—through the manipulation of certain musical elements.

A fourth way to start the music-making is to establish a procedural parameter. One way to begin improvisation experiences with adults who can comprehend language is to ask them to take a moment of silent reflection and start whenever they are moved to begin playing. This allows for each player to ponder how they will contribute to the group experience and determine when they are ready to join the process. Often, the person who plays first has an apparent investment in the process or resulting product. Obviously, if the same player starts each time, there may be issues of impulsivity or control to explore within the group.

Another useful parameter is to specify who will begin on the basis of the instrument they are playing. For example, the leader might direct the players to enter one at a time, beginning with the smallest instrument and ending with the largest in the group. Or the therapist might ask those with shakers to begin and those with strikers and scrapers to join in. One benefit of this type of start (a procedural given) is that reticent or resistant players may be more quickly engaged.

A less structured way to begin an improvisation is to use a gesture that communicates, "Let's begin!" This might be a head nod, a circular or swirling motion with the hand, or a finger point. With a gestural start, control of the tempo, meter, etc., is negotiated among the players rather than assumed by the therapist. On the other hand, gestural starts can be vague and may confuse certain players.

Another possible tactic is to employ a single strike on a gong or cymbal to signal the start of the music-making. In effect, this functions similarly to a gestural start in that no specific rhythmic (and hence, stylistic) elements are predesignated, although the dynamic level could be suggested.

Now it is time for you to practice. (Note: The following exercise is designed to be accomplished in the group as Experiential Learning; however, if you are having difficulty with this particular skill, find a partner for some Independent Skill Development outside of class time.)

Ex 6–1 (Experiential Learning)

Take turns starting improvisations using each of the techniques described above: (1) countdown; (2) "Let's play"; (3) begin playing without speaking; (4) procedural parameter (given); (5) gesture; (6) musical cue. Discuss which types feel least and most comfortable and why. Try to generate at least one new way to begin an improvisation effectively.

Stopping

Stopping a clinical improvisation seems to trigger more anxiety and frustration among students and novice leaders than any other responsibility associated with leadership. Knowing when to stop involves a complex set of decisions based on information, leadership experience, and intuition, and thus lies beyond the scope of this book. I will, however, address how to stop.

As with starting, there will be times that a group improvisation ends naturally. Sometimes it will finish with a loud bang or crash by the ensemble, usually with accompanying smiles, laughter, or shouts; or perhaps it will fizzle out or slow to a stop with sighs, tears, or blank stares. Sometimes a natural ending will feel satisfying or invigorating; at other times it will feel unfinished or disappointing. Just as there may be players who start consistently, there may also be individuals in the group who always have to have "the last word" as the music comes to a close. There may also be individuals who are reluctant to stop—perhaps because they are really enjoying the experience or because a need is yet unfulfilled—even when the allotted time is up, the music has lost its vigor or meaning, or the players are exhausted!

When the guidance of a therapist is required, she or he needs to be ready with a pocketful of tactics to end the music. You will notice that there are similarities between techniques for starting and those for stopping; that is, some are verbal, some are gestural, and some are tied to a procedural given. For instance, one way to end an improvisation is to use a countdown. As with the countdown start, this type of ending puts the authority squarely in the hands of the therapist. Players are expected to stop whether they are ready or not. When employing a countdown stop, the therapist typically calls out a given number and proceeds backwards. For instance, the therapist will say "Four!" at the beginning of a musical phrase, "Three!" at the start of the next phrase, and so on, until the players have reached the downbeat immediately following the final counted phrase. Countdown stops are obviously ill-suited to nonrhythmic improvisations.

Another verbal technique is simply to say, "...and stop." This will usually put an immediate halt to the music and therefore might be indicated when players are *perseverating* (engaging in nonpurposeful, repetitive actions) or acting in an injurious manner. Although effective, this tactic can feel unnaturally abrupt and awkward.

Gestural stops can be difficult to master but quite effective clinically. One of the nice things about nonverbal stops is that they allow the music to continue to conclusion without verbal interference. Some possible hand gestures are (1) a group cutoff (as in formal conducting), (2) a gradual elimination of players in the group with a wave of the hand, (3) the raising of both arms above the head to signal a bombastic ending, and (4) the opposite, a steady decrescendo that eventually leads to silence, accomplished by bringing one or both hands, palms down, from high to low in front of the players. You will find that all of these hand gestures are more effective when the body and face are involved and congruent. With certain clients, gestures will need to be exaggerated; for instance, when working with children or clients who have cognitive impairments, the therapist may begin a decrescendo gesture standing on her or his feet and end with the body crouched down and hands on the floor.

Musical signals, such as a cymbal crash, are useful to stop as well as to start an improvisation. Any instrument can be used to provide the cue, as long as the players are aware of what the signal means and the instrument has enough dynamic potential to cut through very loud music should this be required.

Ex 6–2 (Experiential Learning)

Take turns stopping improvisations using each of the techniques described above: (1) countdown; (2) "Stop!"; (3) gesture; (4) musical cue. Discuss which types feel least and most comfortable. Try to generate at least one new way to stop an improvisation effectively.

COMMUNICATING DURING IMPROVISATION

Competencies addressed in this section include the ability to:

NM 2   *Communicate with players nonverbally while improvising.*
NM 3   *Communicate with players verbally while improvising.*

At times, a therapist may find it necessary to communicate with clients without disrupting or halting the music-making. The above competencies speak to the development of communicative techniques for use while the music proceeds. Gestural (nonverbal) techniques are indicated when (1) the music is so loud that the therapist can not project her or his voice above it, (2) speaking out loud would distract or startle the players, or (3) speaking would upset the character or mood of the music, as during a particularly contemplative or tender passage. Gesture may also be more effective than words when the therapist wants to communicate with one player or a small group within the larger group. Gestures that you will need generally fall into the categories of *encouragement* and *direction* or *redirection*.

Gestures of encouragement are used to communicate pleasure, support, or validation to the clients as they are playing. Smiles, head nods, thumbs up, proximity, and gentle touch fall into this category. Gestures of direction or redirection function to communicate musical and interpersonal action or change that the therapist wants to encourage or require. Some examples are standing up to draw attention to oneself as the leader, moving next to a particular player or closer to an individual to influence their responses, handing someone an instrument to play, adding or eliminating instruments to the improvisation as it continues, pointing to certain individuals when it is their turn to play, and conducting the expressive features of the music, such as tempo, phrasing, and dynamics. Novice leaders need to be reminded that they ought not feel bound to their chairs when they feel the urge to move about, as long as their movement is purposeful and not disruptive. Needless to say, it is essential that every therapist develop clarity and comfort of movement in order to employ communicative gesture in an effective way.

Sometimes the therapist may need to speak to clients while they are improvising. Words are usually more effective than gestures when visibility is obstructed, such as with large groups, and with players who have visual impairments or who close their eyes while improvising (which happens surprisingly often). Therapists often use words in tandem with gesture to make a clearer, more immediate, or more emphatic statement. Brevity is key.

As with gesture, *verbal prompts* function to offer encouragement and direction or redirection. Words of support and encouragement include "Yes," "Good for you," "Keep going," "I like that," "That's beautiful," and "Try again." Words of direction or redirection include "Listen," "Go," "Stop," "Watch me," and "Get ready."

You will find at times that it is necessary for you to give or repeat brief directions, communicate a given, or even converse with a client while continuing to play your instrument. This requires considerable skill! If the music is rhythmic, the tendency for many leaders is either to speak in synchrony with the musical rhythms or in awkward spurts, rather than with the natural prosody of speech. Here is a chance for you to practice talking while playing.

Ex 6–3 (Experiential Learning)

Take turns facilitating a group improvisation. Practice using gesture to "conduct" the expressive features of the music.

Ex 6–4 (Experiential Learning)

While playing a rhythmic improvisation, hold a conversation that involves all members of the group. Ask and answer questions about what is happening in the improvisation. Start with short phrases and sentences and move to longer, more complicated verbalizations. Keep the pulse, tempo, and meter steady!

MOVEMENT

Competencies addressed in this section include the ability to:

NM 4 Move within and around the group while improvising for purposes of support or guidance.

One of the most difficult and uncomfortable challenges for novice leaders is to incorporate their entire physical selves into the process of facilitation. Their uneasiness seems related both to a lack of comfort with their own bodies and an inability to sense when it is prudent to move or how to use movement in an effective manner. I have already alluded to a few situations in which a therapist will find it necessary to move the entire body while improvising, namely during stops and starts and as a way to communicate support and direction without using words. There are at least two other conditions in which you will need to move your entire body. These are addressed in this next competency.

There will be times when you need to move in order to provide general support to one or many players. An example of providing musical support is moving toward and standing or kneeling next to or in front of a player to model or reinforce a particular tempo, rhythm, phrase structure, dynamic level, playing configuration, etc. At times it may be important to draw the group's visual and auditory awareness to a certain player with your physical presence, such as when an otherwise withdrawn adult engages in the improvisation or when a child has mastered a particularly complicated instrument, rhythm, etc., and deserves some recognition. The therapist's physical *proximity*, or nearness, sometimes serves to alter the players' responses in a meaningful and fruitful way. Examples include moving between children to stop counterproductive or harmful interactions, and moving next to an individual as a way to refocus her or his attention or music-making.

Ex 6–5 (Experiential Learning)

Take turns moving about the group during an improvisation: Stand, move to a player, and kneel next to or in front of this person in order to provide support or supervision. Provide feedback to one another about which actions were most helpful.

PHYSICAL ASSISTANCE

Competencies addressed in this section include the ability to:

NM 5   *Help the players produce sound on the percussion instruments as necessary (e.g., position the instrument, hold the instrument, provide hand-over-hand assistance).*

Once you are comfortable moving about the group, you will be able to offer physical assistance to those clients who require it in order to make music. This is the focus of the final competency. (Obviously, physical assistance is not unique to the method of clinical improvisation; you may also need to assist clients in re-creative experiences in which musical instruments are used.) At times, you will reposition an instrument so that it is easier for a client to play or so that it produces a more pleasing sound. At other times, you will be called upon to hold a client's instrument while she or he strikes or scrapes it. Finally, there will be times when you will need to provide direct, *hand-over-hand* assistance so that the client can produce a particular movement to sound the instrument. Following is a case example that may help you think through how you might best physically assist several clients with a range of abilities.

Vignette 6–1

Imagine that you are just starting to use improvisation with a group of children who have various physical disabilities. One child in the group has mild cerebral palsy and has chosen to play the djembe on the stand.

She will not need physical assistance to sound the instrument, but it must be placed a bit to her side rather than directly in front of her in order to accommodate her natural posture and movement patterns. Another child has spina bifida and has selected the maracas. Her upper body is fully functional, so she will require no assistance. A third child has severe cerebral palsy, and his hands and arms are rigidly contracted. He has selected his favorite instrument, a frame drum, for the upcoming improvisation. He is able to grasp the shaft of a mallet with his left hand and has enough range of motion to strike the drum independently. He is not able to hold the drum, nor is he able to balance it on his legs. You could suggest that he position the drum on his wheelchair tray, but that will create an awkward playing position, the drum will certainly slide, and the sound will be muffled and displeasing, unless it is specially constructed to rest on the tray. You will likely need to hold the instrument for him or coach another individual in the room to do likewise.

You know that it is critical to attend to both height and angle as you hold the frame drum. One possible error would be holding the instrument too high, especially if you are standing in front of the seated client, which is not recommended but which may be unavoidable at times. Another tendency would be for you to hold the drum perpendicular or parallel to the floor, neither of which would be a fitting angle for most players. You will need to assess this child's natural arc of movement in order to determine the best angle for him. Finally, you will need to hold the instrument in such a way that you provide the necessary resistance to the force of his beating. If the drum "flops" when the child attempts to play it, he may modify his playing unnecessarily or become frustrated and give up.

The last child in the group is a boy with multiple and severe physical and sensory impairments. He has no speech and no discernable functional movement of his limbs, which are flaccid. You are not sure how much he is able to see, but you know that he tracks purposefully with his eyes and can produce a head nod in response to yes-no questions. Using his eyes or head to communicate, he can select his own instrument; however, he will need hand-over-hand assistance in order to play it, unless he is able to use the functional movement of his head to play an adapted instrument. (If you have never provided hand-over-hand assistance to an individual, it would be wise to talk with teachers, parents, physical therapists, and occupational therapists who know this child and his particular physical needs and objectives.) In most situations, it is possible to provide gentle physical assistance without risk of causing pain or physical damage. Fortunately, you have been in the classroom while the physical therapist assists this child in holding and using a spoon during lunch. You have noticed that she sits beside him and supports his elbow joint with one hand and his grasping hand with another. Using this same principle, you may be able to support his elbow and hand so that he can strike a drum with a mallet. It probably would not be prudent to use a small drum; a large target will afford more success in this situation.

Ex 6–6 (Didactic Learning)

With a partner, play your collection of strikers, shakers, and scrapers one at a time. Take turns repositioning and holding the instruments for the other player. Pay attention to height, angle, and the strength required to balance the other individual's playing force. Discuss your findings in the group.

Ex 6–7 (Experiential Learning)

In the context of a group improvisation, designate two or three individuals to provide hand-over-hand assistance to other players. Repeat until all group members have had an opportunity to assist other "clients." Discuss.

Vocabulary for Chapter Six

1. *Verbalizations*
2. *Gestures*
3. *Countdown*
4. *Perseverating*
5. *Encouragement/Praise*
6. *Direction/Redirection*
7. *Verbal Prompts*
8. *Proximity*

9.   *Hand-over-Hand*

Chapter Seven

MUSICAL FACILITATION SKILLS

Thus far, you have been introduced to the terms and nomenclature relevant to clinical improvisation, as well as the musical elements that you will employ. You have explored the instruments and experimented with their unique sounds and inherent challenges. In Chapter Five, you learned about the importance of structure in group improvisation and practiced developing suitable session structures. You then moved on to the verbal and gestural facilitative processes. Now you have arrived at what I believe are the most interesting and unique of all procedures and techniques in our toolbox: *musical facilitation* techniques.

Unfortunately, as I have already noted in Chapter Two, there is great disparity in the terms used to describe the processes and products of clinical improvisation. The musical facilitation techniques are no exception. In many writings, techniques are named yet remain undefined or untethered to any kind of classification system, leading to ambiguity. Synonyms are erroneously used, leading to confusion. For example, synchrony, an empathic technique (Bruscia, 1987), is alternately referred to in the literature as "joining" and "matching." However, "matching" is also used synonymously or in conjunction with "reflecting" (Robbins & Robbins, 1991) and as a form of "mirroring" (Pavlicevic, 1997). Wigram (2004) writes:

> *Mirroring* and *imitating* are frequently used as empathic techniques where the music therapist intends to give a message to the client that they are meeting them exactly at their level and attempting to achieve synchronicity with the client (p. 82).

Are we then to assume that mirroring, imitating, meeting, and synchronizing refer to the same technique? Here is another example of linguistic mishandling:

> At first [the client] was unaware of Helen's presence at the piano, as she joined his tempo of beating and matched his vocal sounds,

> hoping to make a connection. ... Helen was here using the techniques described earlier, similar to those used when a mother, listening and attending to her baby, matches and imitates the sounds that the baby makes. (Darnley-Smith & Patey, 2003, p. 99)

From this excerpt, one might conclude that joining, matching, and imitating refer to the same set of actions by the therapist, yet this may not be the intended meaning.

Bruscia (1987) has developed what I believe is a comprehensible and comprehensive taxonomy of techniques that helps to unshroud some of the mystery related to this important feature of clinical work. Bruscia has organized the techniques (both musical and nonmusical) into nine distinct categories: *Empathy, Structuring, Elicitation, Redirection, Intimacy, Procedural, Referential, Emotional Exploration,* and *Discussion.* Of his list, I have selected exclusively from the musical techniques, versus techniques in other modalities—verbal, art, etc. (Discussion techniques, which usually occur after the improvisation has occurred, will be addressed in Chapter Nine.) In this chapter, you will read about and practice several musical facilitation techniques that I believe have relevance for entry-level clinical practice. You will also be cursorily introduced to more advanced techniques that most music therapists would position within the realm of music psychotherapy or insight-oriented therapy (Wheeler, 1983). I believe it is important that all clinicians are aware of some of these advanced techniques, but additional training in improvisation as a form of music psychotherapy is strongly advised in order that facilitators can develop a thorough understanding of treatment indications and contraindications and the confidence necessary to use these advanced techniques effectively and ethically.

Clinical citations accompany most techniques. The majority of these illustrations hail from literature connected to the practice of dyadic improvisation; this is due to the aforementioned paucity of published text on the use of improvisation with client groups and, specifically, the use of clinical techniques in the context of group therapy. In spite of the fact that many of the examples do not reflect a group emphasis, all of the techniques presented below are pertinent to group improvisation and can be quite potent in this milieu. And, although the focus here is on clinical skills, the general music education students who have completed the improvisation course have found many of these techniques to be of great value in public and private school settings with typically developing children and adolescents.

I would like to make three points about the techniques. The first is that, although the techniques are neatly categorized here, Bruscia indicates that they do overlap with one another more often than not. In many cases, they serve similar functions, and they are typically used in combination with one another, both simultaneously and consecutively within improvisation experiences and sessions.

The second point is that, in one sense, the techniques that you choose to employ within the context of group improvisation are often suggestive of a role that you are assuming. For instance, as you will see, one of the choices that you may make is to provide a rhythmic or tonal ground for the group's music-making. In this sense, you are establishing yourself as a consistent presence upon whom the players can rely and, depending upon the level of organization among the various players, the "glue" that binds the group's expressions. On the other hand, you may choose to recede from an improvisation and allow the group to continue playing on its own. In the latter situation, you are establishing yourself as a different kind of leader, one who encourages the players to explore their own strengths and who trusts them to find their own structures, all the while remaining available to them should they require your intervention. Nolan (2003) points to this incontrovertible connection between actions and the therapist's role in his description of improvisational work with a young man:

> During all of the musical experiences, I took various positions as accompanist, co-creator, and/or initiator, in different musical pieces or within the same piece, while maintaining my role as therapist. Sometimes, especially in the early stages of treatment, my musical presence functioned in a similar way to Bolla's description of the transformational mother, in shaping or exerting musical structure in the form of style, and in the determination of many musical elements. Other times, I provided a support by accepting whatever expression in musical sound, "spoken word," or chanted formats emerged. Musically, I

matched the energy level and "fanned the flames" of primal musical expression, or confronted/challenged [the client's] various efforts and expressions directed toward the object of transference. ... At times, my musical function was influenced by my imagined manifestation of what he was attempting to create through me. At other times, my role reflected where, developmentally, he needed, and seemed equipped, or capable, to go. (p. 327)

Finally, the techniques are not meant to be prescriptive, as such. They are used according to what you detect to be the needs and objectives of the group members via your prior knowledge and in-the-moment listening and observation. For now, let us simply become familiar with the various techniques themselves.

TECHNIQUES OF EMPATHY

Competencies addressed in this section include the ability to:

MU 1   Imitate a client's response.
MU 2   Synchronize with a client's playing.
MU 3   Incorporate a musical motif of the client into one's improvising.
MU 4   Pace one's improvising with the client's energy level.
MU 5   Reflect the moods, attitudes, and feelings exhibited by the client.

Empathic techniques can be described as those in-the-moment actions taken by the therapist for the purposes of establishing rapport with the clients, eliciting interaction, and conveying empathy (Bruscia, 1987). Empathy can be defined as "the ability to understand and share the feelings of another" (*The New Oxford American Dictionary,* 2001, p. 557). Techniques of empathy can be useful at all stages of the therapeutic process, but have obvious utility in initial phases or during points of client mistrust, withdrawal, or regression.

Imitating

The first technique of empathy is called *imitation*. This refers to echoing some aspect (rhythmic, tonal, etc.) of the clients' playing after they have played it. When you imitate one or many clients within the context of a group, there are several possible positive outcomes. First, the individual client may gain greater awareness of what she or he is doing in that moment. Second, the other players may also become more aware of the individual or individuals who are being imitated, which can promote their status within the group. Third, the clients may feel as though their musical contributions have been endorsed. A fourth potential benefit is that the clients may accept a position of leadership as they create sounds and you (or other players) emulate them. In his overview of the Paraverbal Therapy model of Heimlich, Bruscia (1987) notes that imitation is frequently used as a clinical technique to encourage interaction, demonstrate cause-effect relationships, and provide sensory feedback. (Note: Imitation, as all of these techniques, must be used cautiously. If imitation is employed too often or for too long a period, clients may feel mimicked or derided rather than esteemed, leading to anger, embarrassment, etc. The clients may also feel unwanted pressure to perform if placed constantly in the leadership role.)

Before proceeding to Exercise 7–3, which focuses more on the natural, clinical use of imitation, let us practice foundational imitation skills in a methodical way.

Ex 7–1 (Experiential Learning)

One person begins by playing a rhythmic or tonal solo consisting of two phrases of a predesignated length. The entire group imitates the second of the two phrases, and the soloing continues with the next player in the circle. Maintain a steady pulse and consistent meter throughout this exercise. Gradually expand the length of the solo and imitation. Which types of phrases were easiest or toughest to copy and why?

Ex 7–2 (Experiential Learning)

Repeat the previous exercise, playing in a nonrhythmic fashion, but in identifiable phrases. Discuss the implications of and differences between imitation in this context and imitation in the previous context.

Ex 7–3 (Experiential Learning)

In round-robin fashion, designate two individuals to serve as co-therapists during a group improvisation. The co-therapists will respond imitatively to each of the other players in an organic fashion, that is, as certain sounds and actions come into awareness. Audio-record and listen. Discuss the exercise. How did it feel to imitate others? What were the challenges? How did it feel to be imitated? Did the use of this technique have any positive or negative outcomes?

Synchronizing

Simply put, *synchrony* refers to doing "what the client does as the client is doing it" (Bruscia, 1987, p. 538). This may mean playing the same rhythmic pattern, melody, harmonic progression, timbre, texture, etc., coincidentally with the clients. It can also mean improvising in synchrony with the clients' movement, breath, etc. Darnley-Smith and Patey (2003) provide a good example of this in their account of a group session with three young children with cerebral palsy:

> After this, Robin moves to the piano as the children take turns to play a large tambourine, held for them by Christine. Mary plays with big, random, and uncontrolled arm movements, which Robin supports with dramatic chords on the piano, timed to coincide with her hand making contact with the tambourine. Gradually, her beating becomes more controlled, and she finds a regular pulse so that she and Robin are playing in time together. (p. 96)

Forinash also refers to the intuitive use of synchrony in her story of improvisation with a hospice patient (Forinash & Gonzalez, 1989):

> The music reflected the change [in her]. I improvised, basing the rhythm on Sara's breathing. As her breaths became more shallow and slower, I changed to softer and slower music (p. 42).

In this example, synchrony of tempo and volume served to create a connection with the client and communicate that, even in her dying moments, the music (and the therapist) was present with her in a very real and physical sense. In group improvisation, the primary purpose of a therapist's synchronizing is to encourage the client's self-awareness and leadership (as with imitation), increase interpersonal and intermusical intimacy, and convey acceptance and empathy to the client (Bruscia, 1987). Bruscia defines *mirroring* as synchrony of action that occurs in reverse direction, such as when the therapist coincides in descent to a client's ascending melody. (Note: If synchronizing is misused or overused, the clients may feel as though they have been invaded by the therapist, and their sense of individuality may be compromised.)

Again, let us practice the skill of synchronizing with others in a methodical fashion, and then we will proceed to a more natural use of the clinical technique.

Ex 7–4 (Experiential Learning)

Take turns synchronizing with a partner's rhythmic or tonal improvisation. Discuss the inherent challenges of this technique.

Ex 7–5 (Experiential Learning)

In round-robin fashion, designate two individuals to serve as co-therapists during a group improvisation. The co-therapists will respond synchronously to each of the other players in an organic fashion, that is, as certain sounds and actions come into awareness. Audio-record and listen. Discuss the exercise. How did it feel to synchronize with others? How did it feel to be synchronized with? What were the challenges? Did the technique have any positive or negative outcomes?

Incorporating

To incorporate means to borrow a motif from the clients' improvisation and integrate it into your own playing (Bruscia, 1987). In contrast to imitation, in which you attempt to play the clients' music verbatim (rhythm for rhythm and/or pitch for pitch), when you incorporate, you may play only a portion of the clients' motifs, alter the patterns in some way, use them when they are first presented, or integrate them into a subsequent improvisation. As an empathic technique, incorporation is designed to communicate acceptance of the clients' musical ideas. It also serves to build repertoire and model musical expression, effort, and resolution. Wigram (2004) accurately asserts that

> The development of a musical relationship through music based on an idea or "theme" presented by the client relies on the therapist's skill in both nurturing as well as exploiting musical material produced by the client (p. 178).

and that themes "... become part of the musical language that builds up, underpinning a shared musical understanding that connects and intensifies the relationship" (p. 179). (Note: When overused or ill-timed, incorporation can leave the clients feeling threatened or cheated, as if you have stolen something personal from them, or mocked, as revealed in the following excerpt:

> Toni often felt that I was "mocking" her in my playing. This happened when I picked up some aspect of her metallophone playing, a harmonic motif, interval or rhythmic fragment, and incorporated it in my piano playing in some way. It was as if Toni had no boundaries between herself and others, she was unable to regulate her experience with the external world. (Loth, 2002, pp. 101–102)

Ex 7–6 (Independent Skill Development)

With a partner, take turns incorporating rhythmic and/or melodic themes that emerge in each other's playing. Audio-record and listen. How well did you do? Was the incorporation evident to your partner during the music-making?

Pacing

The technique of *pacing* requires that you match the clients' level of energy during the improvisation (Bruscia, 1987), in most cases responding to either the intensity (dynamics) or speed (tempo) of the playing. Pacing does not require actions that are identical to those of the clients; only the vigor and phrasing of the actions is matched. Effectively used, pacing can encourage the clients' physical relatedness to their surroundings, promote self-awareness, and ready the clients for a shift in energy.

Ex 7–7 (Experiential Learning)

Designate one person to begin the improvisation as if she or he were a client. The other group members match that player's intensity, speed, and phrasing. Solicit feedback from the "client." Repeat until all members have had a turn to play each role.

Reflecting

As with the other techniques of empathy, reflecting is designed to "convey acceptance of the client's actions and feelings" (Bruscia, 1987, p. 541), demonstrate understanding, and establish a working alliance. Reflection involves expressing the same moods or feelings that the clients are expressing while the clients are expressing them. Unlike imitation and incorporation, the therapist does not necessarily use the same musical elements or materials that the clients are using; instead, the aim is to match the underlying *emotional character* of the clients' actions. Your ability to reflect thus depends upon your ability to "interpret the feelings underlying the client's expression and to translate them into impressions" (p. 541). Henderson (1991) captures the essence of this technique in her poignant account of her work with a severely abused and fragile South African 13-year-old:

> I interpreted her improvisation, which was in 6/8 time, as an expression of her need for comfort, and I began to improvise an African lullaby. Our interaction continued for quite a while and she finally whispered that she was scared. I kept supporting her musically, reflecting the mood she was projecting (p. 214).

Ex 7–8 (Experiential Learning)

Repeat the above exercise, this time reflecting the emotional character of the player's music. What are the challenges here? Does reflecting interface with other techniques? If so, which ones and how?

STRUCTURING TECHNIQUES

Competencies addressed in this section include the ability to:

MU 6   *Establish and maintain a rhythmic ground.*
MU 7   *Establish and maintain a tonal center.*

At times, you may need to provide some kind of structure for your clients' music-making. Bruscia defines three structuring techniques, two of which are discussed here. Miller (1991) writes about her deliberate use of both of these with a group of patients who had long-term mental illness:

> I have found that the best way for the group to function is to allow things to develop, and to provide musical structures at times when this seems appropriate. I provided such structure much more frequently in the first phase of the group process than in later ones, for at the beginning, the group was in the process of finding out about possibilities of using instruments, and some members could participate only with rhythmic or harmonic support from me. (p. 424)

Rhythmic Grounding

One of the most important roles that you will accept or assert as a leader is that of providing a *rhythmic ground* for the other players. Bruscia defines rhythmic grounding as "keeping a basic beat or providing a rhythmic foundation for the client's improvising" (p. 535). A ground supports the temporal organization and stabilization of the music and thus can provide vital safety and security for groups that are disorganized, confused, anxious, or even frantic. This technique also helps players control impulses, remain in physical reality, and gain confidence to express themselves more creatively, as in the following example of an improvisation with an older adult who had Alzheimer's Disease:

> [Sheila] chose a drum and began to play, accompanied by Rachel on the cello. ... After some experimenting, Rachel began to play a continuous, slow, walking rhythm, rather like a ground bass, in the tempo of Sheila's playing. This simple repetitive musical structure enabled Sheila to feel confident enough to continue with her playing and gradually to experiment with the different sounds she could make on the drum. (Darnley-Smith & Patey, 2003, p. 77)

A rhythmic ground is often a basic pulse; it also can be a rhythmic ostinato. Keeping a steady beat on a drum sounds easy enough, but many therapists have difficulty with this most fundamental of rhythmic skills, particularly if their musical training has not required any type of manual coordination. In all players, both skilled and unskilled, there is a tendency toward irregularity of the pulse at times of transition between meters and at the extreme ends of the spectrum of tempi; in the later case, therapists are likely to either drag the tempo when playing very slowly or rush it when playing very quickly. Therefore, it may be beneficial to devote independent practice time to this skill area. Do not shy away from using a metronome while you practice; on the other hand, do not become entirely dependent upon it to establish or maintain the beat. As a music therapist, you will need to develop a confident, internal sense of pulse to guide you in your work, especially if that work is improvisational!

Any time you act as a rhythmic ground during improvisation, it is critical that your pulse is clearly discernable. Consider the notion that certain instruments provide a more precise sound than others. In general, instruments that are struck with the hand or a mallet are more discrete than those that are shaken or scraped. Case in point, contrast the sound of a djembe with that of a cabasa. If you find yourself with an instrument that does not naturally produce a crisp beat and this is what you need to provide, think about how you might adapt your playing to obtain the desired sound. For example, you might find that holding a maraca around the round chamber as opposed to the handle allows you to produce a more precise movement and therefore a more distinct pulse. Likewise, tapping the rim of a nonheaded tambourine on the palm of the opposite hand obviously produces a more discrete sound than shaking the instrument in the air. (Note: Rhythmic grounding must be used carefully so as not to restrict the clients' musical expression. Along these lines, Wigram cautions against imposing meter: "In fact, it can be quite constraining and directive to take the client's musical production and establish a specific metre such as 4/4 or 3/4 for what they are doing" [2004, p. 93]).

Ex 7–9 (Experiential Learning)

In duple and triple meter and in a variety of tempi, take turns establishing and maintaining rhythmic grounds. Use both basic pulse and rhythmic ostinati. How does it feel to provide the primary rhythmic structure for the group?

Ex 7–10 (Experiential Learning)

A fun challenge within this competency is for some players to take turns holding the rhythmic ground steady while the others purposefully attempt to throw it off. (Your clients may try the same thing!)

Tonal Centering

Centering works much the same way as the rhythmic ground, except that the elements employed are tonal. Here, the therapist "grounds" and contains the clients' playing in a key center, scale, or harmonic component (Bruscia, 1987), as the following metaphor by Darnley-Smith and Patey (2003) suggests:

> In an adult mental health setting, the music of a new group of patients, who were acutely ill, was extremely chaotic. Some were playing music which was loud and energetic, whilst others were quietly experimenting. ... The therapist felt an urgent need to provide some structure. She began to play a simple three-chord progression on the piano, at first starting with single notes, and then gradually building up the chords so that they became more

complex....She used the sounds she was making as a means of providing a musical focus, a   point of safety, leadership, and containment. It was as though she was a mother putting down a large mat in a nursery upon which all the children could play together. Gradually the patients' sounds became less disparate and more connected as they began to respond to the security of the musical structure that the therapist was providing. (p. 81)

In a more succinct fashion, Robarts (2004) describes centering through the use of a harmonic vamp in her sessions with a severely abused 11 year-old girl:

I answer her musings about music therapy leading into a gentle I Ib IV V accompaniment—banal in its predictability, wherein lies its therapeutic value in this instance. It becomes a refrain, to which we return, when the musical development of emotional expression is more than Lena can bear ... .(p. 158)

Ex 7–11 (Experiential Learning)

Repeat the above exercise, substituting tonal centering. How does it feel to provide the primary tonal structure for the group?

ELICITATION TECHNIQUES

Competencies addressed in this section include the ability to:

MU 8   Use repetition as an invitation for the client to respond.
MU 9   Model desired musical responses.
MU 10 Make spaces in one's improvising for the client's improvising.
MU 11 Interject music into the spaces made by the client.

This set of in-the-moment actions is performed by the therapist in order to bring something forth from the client.

Repeating

In repeating, a rhythmic or tonal motif from the clients' or therapist's music-making is repeated by the therapist in order to elicit a response from the client and/or establish a mood in the improvisation (Bruscia, 1987). Typically, repetition of a motif ends with a distinctive musical rest, which functions as an invitation for response.

Ex 7–12 (Independent Skill Development)

With a partner, practice repeating as an elicitation technique. Did you find specific ways to facilitate your partner's response?

Modeling

Here, modeling involves the therapist demonstrating a desired musical response, such as a playing technique on a specific instrument or a musical motif (Bruscia, 1987). Montello (2004) used modeling with a traumatized client to elicit courage to improvise vocally:

> During this phase of treatment, Jennifer was dealing with feelings of alienation from her body, heart, and soul. As a way of making contact with her deeper self, I encouraged Jennifer to engage in vocal improvisations with me at the piano. She was terrified of opening her mouth and singing. In a playful way, I demonstrated my own style of vocal improvisation. "Why are you having so much fun?" she asked me. (p. 311)

Ex 7–13 (Experiential Learning)

Take turns modeling desired musical responses for the group members. The responses can be rhythmic, tonal, or relate to the use of particular instruments (including the voice). Discuss.

Making Spaces

In this elicitation technique, the therapist stops playing momentarily and allows the client to fill in the silence with her or his music (Bruscia,

1987). The primary purpose of making spaces is to elicit a musical response, as is evident in the following excerpt by Smeijsters (2005):

> Van den Hurk, in her improvisations with the client, used techniques of "elicitation" and "redirection" (Bruscia, 1987). The first type of technique was used to stimulate the client to react. As a result of meter, rhythm, and melodic line and chord progression, a musical process is felt as an ongoing process in time, and an anticipation of good continuation is evoked. While participating in a musical play, one is stimulated to keep it going. If the music therapist leaves an open space in the ongoing process, then the client is provoked to fill up this space, to give an answer to it....In this treatment of Joshua, Van den Hurk gradually introduced open spaces more suddenly. This stimulated Joshua to react spontaneously. (p. 137)

Interjecting

Interjecting can be considered the opposite of leaving spaces, where the therapist musically fills in the spaces left by the client, as in the description provided by Nolan (2004):

> During these [piano] pieces, Rick would occasionally give me solos. He would communicate this by dropping his volume and by removing any melody, limiting the right hand to open intervals in an accompanying style (p. 330).

Ex 7–14 (Independent Skill Development)

With a partner, practice leaving purposeful spaces in your music for her or his interjections. Switch roles.

REDIRECTION TECHNIQUES

Competencies addressed in this section include the ability to:

MU 12 Introduce musical change to redirect the client's playing.
MU 13 Intensify elements within the improvisation.

Introducing Change

In this technique, the therapist introduces new rhythmic or tonal figures in order to move through an impasse or counteract rigidity (Bruscia, 1987). Smeijsters (2005) pens:

> With "redirection" techniques, Van den Hurk introduced new musical motifs, intensified the musical play, and destabilized existing patterns. Joshua was transported into musical territories he had never experienced before. After some time, he himself initiated musical redirections (p. 137).

Ex 7–15 (Experiential Learning)

Take turns in small groups introducing new musical material for the express purpose of destabilizing existing patterns. How did this feel? What were the reactions of the other players?

Intensifying

Amir (1996) describes her use of imitation followed by intensification with a 25-year-old man in psychotherapy:

> I imitated his drumming and slowly brought a little more energy, accelerating the tempo and making louder sounds. He joined me and together we created an improvisation that reached a *forte* (p. 52).

To intensify means to increase or add tension to some aspect of the music (Bruscia, 1987). (Notice that the term itself suggests the word "tense.") In improvisation, the elements that are most frequently intensified are the dynamics and tempo (as in the above example), rhythm patterns, and melody.

Ex 7–16 (Experiential Learning)

In the group, take turns acting as the leader, intensifying some aspect of the sounds that are being created. Which aspect was easiest to intensify and why? Which was most difficult and why?

INTIMACY TECHNIQUES

Competencies addressed in this section include the ability to:

MU 14   *Assist clients in the sharing of instruments.*
MU 15   *Bond with the client through the creation and repetition of a musical theme.*
MU 16   *Demonstrate the effective use of musical soliloquy.*

Techniques designed to promote client-therapist closeness for the purposes of advancing the therapeutic (working) relationship can be termed *intimacy techniques* (Bruscia, 1987).

Sharing Instruments

You may suggest that a client share an instrument with you or with another group member for purposes of promoting intimacy, exploring interpersonal boundaries, and establishing give-and-take in the relationship (Bruscia, 1987). In group therapy, two or more players may share an instrument. Instruments that can be shared comfortably by multiple improvisers (playing simultaneously) are the piano, drum set, bodhran, crash cymbal, large djembe, gathering drum, gong, split drum, temple blocks, and larger (alto or bass) barred instruments. (Note: Some clients may have difficulty sharing an instrument due to a fear of being overcome by the other player or because of boundary ambiguity.)

Ex 7–17 (Experiential Learning)

So that you can experience what your clients may experience, play several improvisations with dyads and triads of players sharing various instruments. Talk about your feelings related to the physical and musical intimacy required in this exercise.

Bonding

Bonding involves the development of a musical theme that represents the therapeutic relationship. The theme may emerge from the therapist's or clients' improvising or both. (Note: Since this technique relates to an ongoing relationship between client and therapist, it is not feasible to practice this technique in the context of these exercises.)

Soliloquy

In a *soliloquy*, the therapist (or client) "improvises a song as if talking to him/herself about the client [him/herself]" (Bruscia, 1987, p. 548). This is akin to what Boxill (1985) terms "identification," a technique that she used regularly in the first stages of therapy with individuals who have developmental disabilities. In this technique, the therapist provides feedback for the client in the form of improvised songs and chants about the client, therapist, situation, and actions of the moment.

Ex 7–18 (Independent Skill Development & Experiential Learning)

With a partner, improvise a rhythm-based (chant) soliloquy (accompanied or a capella) to describe some aspect of your "internal conversation" about the other person. Switch roles. Try out this technique in the larger group, this time improvising about the group as a whole. How comfortable were you with this technique?

PROCEDURAL TECHNIQUES

Competencies addressed in this section include the ability to:

MU 17 Recede from playing during a group improvisation.

Receding

Most of the procedural techniques are nonmusical in nature. One, however, warrants our attention. This is *receding*, in which the therapist pulls back or withdraws completely from improvising with the group (Bruscia, 1987). Your retreat may help clients take more responsibility and express themselves in a freer manner. (Note: A retreat that is unexpected or too sudden may stimulate feelings of abandonment in certain clients.)

Ex 7–19 (Experiential Learning)

In a group of no more than four total players, take turns serving as the group's leader and then receding from the improvisation. As you retreat, pay attention to what happens in the musical and nonmusical responses of the other players. What factors influenced your decision of when to recede? How did it feel to pull out? What did you hear and observe as a listener?

REFERENTIAL TECHNIQUES

Competencies addressed in this section include the ability to:

MU 18 Improvise to a client's free association.

Free Associating

We have already discussed the use of referents as a way to structure improvisations. One technique that we have not yet explored is the use of musical free association. This is a receptive technique in which the therapist improvises to the clients' verbalized associations. It can be used to ready the client for a referential piece or to explore unconscious material that emerges through the free association (Bruscia, 1987). Although not termed *free association*, the essence of this technique is beautifully captured in a case study by Robarts (2004), in which the therapist improvises at the piano in response to the client's spontaneous songs and *Sprächgesang*.

Ex 7–20 (Experiential Learning)

Acting as a therapist, take turns improvising in response to various players' free associations, presented in either verbal or song lyric format. What challenges accompany this technique? How did the "client" respond to your musical interpretation of their words?

EMOTIONAL EXPLORATION TECHNIQUES

The final section in this chapter describes some of the techniques of emotional exploration. All of the techniques in this category are designed to assist the client as she or he explores both previously encountered and in-the-moment emotions. Verbal processing is an integral aspect of these techniques.

Please note that these are advanced techniques for clinicians with advanced training in clinical improvisation. They are not to be used by undergraduate students in music therapy practica; neither are they to be used by seasoned clincians without proper training and supervision, no matter how many years these individuals have been practicing or how skillfully they are able to facilitate other music therapy methods. I include them here solely to heighten the readers' (my students') awareness and stimulate interest in improvisation as a form of music psychotherapy.

Holding

Holding, also called "containing" in the literature, is one of the most frequently cited emotional techniques, and citations appear in publications anchored in a wide variety of theoretical perspectives. Mary Priestley (Analytical Music Therapy) is attributed with the first uses of the term in the context of music psychotherapy. Bruscia defines holding as providing a "musical background or accompaniment that reverberates the client's feelings while also offering a musical structure for containing their release" (1987, p. 552). The technique is used to help the client explore and express or release difficult feelings in a safe and reassuring environment. Although his definition of holding differs from that espoused here, Wigram's "containing" example helps us understand how the therapist's music can serve to "draw a line around" particularly raw expression:

> Containing implies a different process where the client's music is quite chaotic and may also be quite loud. Therapeutically, the client needs to be allowed to be chaotic, noisy, exaggerated (a good example would be an out-of-control child having a "musical/emotional" tantrum). The therapist provides a musical container for the client's music, playing strongly and confidently enough to be heard by the client. ... it needs to be structured music that provides a pattern. (2004, p. 97)

Kowski (2003) describes her use of the holding technique with a group of children who have emotional disturbances:

> I started playing the guitar, strumming D minor, A minor (picking up the pentatonic scale of the marimba phone: FGACD), establishing a   holding environment. I tried to send the signal that I was there to hold (using the AMT "holding technique"), protect and encourage them, and not to stop them unless somebody acted in a destructive manner (pp. 91–92).

Holding is a difficult concept to convey in words yet it is readily identifiable in sound. The reader is referred to Track 32 on Wigram's (2004) companion disc for a dyadic example with percussion instruments.

Doubling

When a therapist (or peer) serves as a double for the client, they express musically (or verbally, through movement, etc.) feelings that the client is unable to clearly or fully articulate. When properly applied, this technique has the effect of expanding the clients' awareness of, expression of, and ownership for their feelings (Bruscia, 1987). Austin (1991) writes about her use of this technique within improvised song with clients who have been traumatized, reflecting through her own solo singing what she senses the clients are feeling in a given moment but are not able or willing to express in sound.

Contrasting

In this technique, the therapist directs the clients to sequentially explore, through improvisation, divergent qualities or feelings (Bruscia, 1987). In most cases, contrasting is accomplished with the use of referents that encapsulate the notions being portrayed. Verbal processing is typically used as a way to help the client synthesize important aspects of the experience of improvising in contrast.

Splitting

In splitting, the therapist and clients simultaneously or alternately improvise the "good" and "bad" parts of a feeling or situation within the client's experience of self (Bruscia, 1987). An example is the intrapersonal split between the "real" and "ideal" self. Often the therapist and clients switch roles and repeat the representation. The splitting technique assists the client in gaining awareness and insight toward the integration of polarities of experience, as in the following example:

> I asked Henry if he could play the music of [himself as] the "awed musician." He improvised a fresh, elegant, yet powerfully sensual line that conveyed a sense of mastery and confidence. I then asked him to play himself in relation to the "awed musician." His music was bland and colorless, lacking in any power or sensuality. The contrast was remarkable. (Montello, 1998, p. 311)

Transferring

In transferring, the therapist and client assume specific roles to help the client explore significant interpersonal and/or familial relationships in her or his life (Bruscia, 1987). Montello (2004) articulates her use of this technique (paired with doubling) and its power with a 32-year-old woman who had been emotionally and physically abused by her mother:

Jennifer had become the mother who ignored, rejected, and abused the innocent "divine child" who simply wanted to play — to love and be loved. We engaged in musical role-playing to explore this dynamic. I played her out-of-control mom and she would defend herself. It was helpful for her to have a chance to fight back. I was moved, however, to take care of the "little girl." During one session when Jennifer was loathe to listen to her "little girl" part, I played her role and during a vocal improvisation, sang, "You're using me, you never let me have any fun. ..." Jennifer was touched by my words. (p. 315)

Vocabulary for Chapter Seven

1. *Techniques of Empathy*
   - *a.*   *imitation*
   - *b.*   *synchrony*
   - *c.*   *mirroring*
   - *d.*   *incorporating*
   - *e.*   *pacing*
   - *f.*   *reflecting*
2. *Structuring Techniques*
   - *a.*   *rhythmic grounding*
   - *b.*   *tonal centering*
3. *Elicitation Techniques*
   - *a.*   *Repeating*
   - *b.*   *modeling*
   - *c.*   *making spaces*
   - *d.*   *interjecting*
4. *Redirection Techniques*
   - *a.*   *introducing change*
   - *b.*   *differentiating*
   - *c.*   *modulating*
   - *d.*   *intensifying*
5. *Intimacy Techniques*
   - *a.*   *sharing instruments*

Chapter Eight

MAKING SENSE OF WHAT WE HEAR: THE IAPs

Vignette 8–1

Imagine that you are a student music therapist who has just begun your clinical training at the local forensic psychiatric hospital. It is Tuesday morning, and seven patients from Unit Five greet you on their way into the therapy room. The chairs in the room are arranged in a circle, and there are varied percussion instruments in the center on the floor.

Once everyone is seated, your supervisor makes introductions and asks each person in the circle to choose an instrument that appeals to them. One by one the participants select an instrument and bring it back to their seats. After a moment of silence, one patient, Bob, begins a moderately-paced pulse on a conga drum. You watch as two other patients join in, playing simple rhythmic patterns in time with the beat. The music therapist and the rest of the players add their sound to the mix, and you begin to play sporadic triplets on your tambourine. Now everyone is improvising together, and your attention turns to the various timbres that are created.

You find yourself drawn first but only briefly to the sound of the temple blocks, and you notice that the patient who is playing them, Chris, is attempting a syncopated rhythm that is slightly misaligned with the underlying pulse of the group. You pick out the sound of the cabasa, and then your focus shifts abruptly to the sound of the bongos and the talking drum. The patients playing these two instruments are improvising imitatively. Another player, Ruth, joins in the "copy game," and all three patients smile at one another. One patient, Karen, is creating lively and syncopated rhythms, but her playing is barely audible and is inconsistent in tempo. She appears disinterested in the entire experience, slouching, leaning her arm on the chair, and avoiding eye contact with the other players. After about a minute of sound, Bob, the player who started the improvisation, ceases the pulse; quite suddenly the rhythmic patterns dissipate, becoming seemingly random thuds and clicks. You start to feel uneasy. Someone punctuates the composite sound with a series of frantic scrapes on the guiro. The sound is harsh and unsettling. The auditory input is beginning to overwhelm you. You don't know what to listen for and, although you continue to play, you are not sure how to make any kind of meaningful contribution to the improvisation.

You will find that one of the most difficult, yet most critical, aspects of the facilitation of group improvisation is listening, the focus of this chapter. How do you know what to listen for? Your attention may wander from player to player or sound to sound, as the above vignette suggests. Sometimes you may focus on your own playing, sometimes on that of another player or subgroup of players, and sometimes on the music of the group as a whole. At certain moments you may be attracted to a particular musical element, such as the timbre, volume level, or tempo of the piece. At other times, you may be attracted to a musical process, such as the accumulation of harmonic tension as time goes by. It is no wonder that even expert facilitators often feel bombarded by the enormity of simultaneous input resulting from group improvisation. And, assuming you are able to settle in and really listen to one precise feature of the music, what words do you use to label it for yourself and talk about it with others?

Some music therapists audio- or video-record group improvisations so that they can review them more carefully after their sessions. Some therapists transcribe the improvisations from these recordings using traditional or nontraditional systems of notation. Recording and transcription can be helpful tools but they can not assist you in "real time," as the music unfolds. Let me suggest an in-the-moment, real-time listening framework that I have found helpful in my clinical work, research, and teaching. This is a system called the Improvisation Assessment Profiles (IAPs), developed by Bruscia (1987). The profiles were originally created as a client assessment tool. In this chapter, we will explore the IAPs as a listening guide and a system of description for both the processes and products of clinical improvisation.

IMPROVISATION ASSESSMENT PROFILES (IAPs)

The IAPs are composed of six profiles, and each profile exists as a way to describe how clients use, organize, manipulate, and combine sound and *musical elements* in their solo playing and in their improvisations with other players. As such, the profiles are a way for us to understand the rhythmic, tonal, textural, dynamic, and timbral relationships that are formed through improvisation. The IAPs also address other significant connections created in improvisation, such as the physical (relationships between the music and aspects of the body), and the programmatic (relationships between the music and images, stories, lyrics, etc.).

The relationships that develop within a single client's music are called *intramusical relationships* (the prefix "intra" means "within"), and the relationships that develop between a client's music and the music of other players are called *intermusical relationships* (the prefix "inter" means "between").

Intramusical Relationships

In the above vignette, as soon as each patient from Unit Five picked up an instrument and began to play, a relationship was initiated. Not only did each player define her or his relationship with the instrument itself (evidenced by choosing it, holding it or positioning it relative to the body, and physically manipulating it in a certain way), but in creating sound, she or he began to form ongoing and audible intramusical relationships. Again, *intramusical relationships* refer to how the various elements employed within the player's music connect with one another. This type of relationship is present every time a person improvises, in solo, dyadic, and group improvisations alike. In our example, as Bob created a pulse on the head of a drum, for instance, he simultaneously employed multiple elements: pulse, tempo, timbre, and volume. What were the evident relationships between these components? Pulse and tempo are always inextricably linked—by definition you can not have one without the other—,but what about tempo and volume? Were there discernable relationships between his tempo and volume? (Often players will increase the loudness level as the speed of the music increases, for example.) What about timbre? Were changes in the timbre of Bob's playing related in any way to changes in tempo and volume? Each of the Unit Five patients organized and manipulated the elements of sound in specific ways, forging various types of internal connections. They formed rhythmic patterns through the use of subdivisions. These subdivisions existed within a metric structure, which was tied to a pulse, which had a given tempo, and so on. These intramusical relationships can be revealed to us through the use of the first five profiles of the IAPs, *Salience, Integration, Variability, Tension,* and *Congruence,* which we will explore below.

Intermusical Relationships

In the case of dyadic or group improvisation, the potential exists for a client to make connections with others through music. For purposes of our discussion, these are, perhaps, the most significant types of relationships to distinguish. Again, we term these *intermusical.* I write that "the potential exists" for these connections to occur because, whereas intramusical relationships are a certainty of every improvisation, intermusical relationships are optional, in a sense. That is, just because a client is improvising within the context of a group does not mean that she or he will necessarily connect with the music of the other players. It is possible for a client to be oblivious to, ignore, and even actively reject musical relationships with other members. We can use the same five profiles that we use to make sense of the intramusical features to understand intermusical features. Bruscia (1987) developed an additional profile, *Autonomy,* which applies exclusively to dyadic or group improvisation, in that it targets role relationships between players, specifically leader and follower roles during the music-making.

The Profiles

Take a look at Appendix F. Here you will see each of the six profiles and their corresponding definitions. For each profile, you will note that five *gradients* exist. These gradients are essentially a continuum of classification, from one extreme to the other, used to describe the player's responses within the profile being addressed. For example, in the *Variability* profile, "Rigid" refers to a player's "persistent maintenance or repetition of a musical element or any of its components—beyond what is commonly accepted as musically meaningful" (Bruscia, 1987, p. 430). At the other extreme, "Random" refers to a total lack of preservation and predictability, with "drastic, frequent, abrupt, and meaningless" changes in the musical materials (Bruscia, 1987, p. 431). Specific definitions for each of the gradients in each of the six profiles can be found in Bruscia's book (1987). Be aware that, in client assessment, the extreme gradients are reserved for extreme situations, and when consistently applied to an individual's improvising, suggesting a tendency, may point to some form of pathology. The relationship between the profiles and gradients will become clearer as we examine each of them in the following sections. Hopefully, the clinical example at the beginning of the chapter will help us make sense of these concepts in context. At the conclusion of each section, you will find additional clinical examples for optional discussion.

SALIENCE. *Competencies addressed in this section include the ability to:*

LI 1   *Define salience.*
LI 2   *Determine what elements and aspects of improvisation are salient at any given time.*

The first profile of the IAPs is termed *Salience*, and it emerges as one of the most important to the listener. Strictly defined, salient means "most noticeable or important" (*The New Oxford American Dictionary*, 2001, p. 1504). The concept of salience will be extremely essential to all subsequent listening processes, because it will act as a triage, helping you to discern and focus on the most prominent and influential features of an improvisation at any given time and ignore or postpone attention to other features. As such, it will serve as a way to delimit and make more manageable that which is heard. The five gradients for this profile serve as a continuum of prominence, from "Receding" (little prominence) to "Overpowering" (obliterating prominence). Without hearing the improvisation described in *Vignette 8–1*, it is impossible to predict what features would have emerged as salient to you, the listener. But it is important to mention here that the absence, as well as the presence, of a particular feature may be what draws the listener's attention (e.g., a lack of musical tension, dynamic contrast, or steady pulse).

As the intern in the example, you listened to the group improvise, and everything you heard and noticed seemed (or sounded) equally important. In other words, every sound appeared in the foreground, on the right side of the gradient continuum ("overpowering"). You felt your attention pulled in many different directions and had difficulty maintaining your aural focus on any one aspect for a notable length of time. As a result, listening and understanding was fragmented. The concept of salience could have helped you make deliberate decisions about what aspects of the improvisation warranted rigorous attention, and for how long.

Think about the concept of salience and how this profile relates to intramusical and intermusical relationships in improvisation. At any given time in a group improvisation, either one might dominate your awareness. As the listener in the vignette above, were you drawn more to what was happening *within* each patient's improvising or what was occurring in the musical exchanges *between* the players? Or, did your attention vacillate? Let us take a moment to consider the possibilities.

As you listened to Karen, the "disinterested woman," you were primarily focused on the intramusical aspects of her improvisation. You noticed that Karen's playing was "lively and syncopated" (the music had some rhythmic vitality), yet the sounds were "barely audible" (so low in volume that they could hardly be heard) and the tempo of her playing was erratic. Without realizing it, perhaps, you were making some important observations about the relationship between the rhythmic, dynamic, and temporal aspects of her creation, and you sensed that something was amiss. This player stood out in your perceptual field because there was an oddity in the way she internally organized and manipulated the musical elements.

Had you chosen to, you might have tuned into the intermusical aspects of Karen's playing, either in place of or in addition to the intramusical relationships that you discerned. How did features of her playing, specifically pulse, tempo, and dynamics, relate to these same elements as created by the patients around her? The point here is that, although certain facets of an improvisation may emerge and command your attention during the listening process, you will need to make constant and deliberate decisions to either remain focused on these facets or let your consciousness expand to take in additional facets. These decisions are based, in part, on your *listening set*. Here, "listening set" is defined as the sum total of the contextual information and biases with which you enter the improvisational process. As a new intern, your listening set might have been quite limited—let us assume that you had been given only scant information about each of the patients and a brief notion of the clinical purpose of the improvisation experience. Your supervisor, on the other hand, had a more complete and precise listening set. She wanted to see if and how improvisation might stimulate communication between certain members of the group, members who have until this point been withdrawn and somewhat resistant to group music-making of any kind. She was particularly interested in how Ruth, Karen, and another patient would relate to one another through the music experience. Her listening set was thus shaped by her objective to assess interpatient communication; naturally, her listening would have an intermusical orientation.

Additional Example: A few players in the improvisation group beat the drums so loudly that the volume obscures all other features present in the music, such as the syncopated rhythms that one member plays on the agogo bells and the pentatonic melody that another plays on the temple blocks. In this case, the scale of "volume" might be considered overpowering, and the other scales, "rhythmic figure" and "melodic," might be considered receding. (intermusical).

Now it is time for you to practice listening with the concept of salience in mind. As you work through the following exercises, trust your first instincts.

Ex 8–1: Salience (Experiential Learning)

One group member improvises while the others listen. Stop the player periodically and check in with the listeners: What is the most dominant, noticeable, or controlling feature of the improvisation at the moment it was halted? Is there some consensus among the listeners?

Ex 8–2: Salience (Experiential Learning)

Repeat Ex 8–1 with multiple players using identical instruments. How is the experience of listening to one player different from listening to more than one?

Ex 8–3: Salience (Experiential Learning)

Repeat Ex 8–1 with multiple players using a variety of percussion and tonal instruments. How is this experience different from Ex 8–2?

INTEGRATION. *Competencies addressed in this section include the ability to:*

LI 3   *Define Integration.*
LI 4   *Determine levels of integration for rhythmic, tonal, textural, dynamic, and timbral elements.*

The second profile in the IAPs is termed *Integration*. To integrate means "to combine two or more things together so that they become a whole" (*The New Oxford American Dictionary*, 2001, p. 882). In the context of improvisation, integration refers to the degree of organization and alignment that the therapist hears as she or he listens to simultaneous features of the music. Another way to think of this profile is as the relationship between all vertical aspects of the improvisation, as laid out in an orchestral score.

We have already discussed the terms "figure" and "ground" as they apply to rhythmic and tonal elements. Rhythmic and tonal *figure-ground* relationships figure prominently in the Integration profile. A rhythmic figure-ground relationship is evident when subdivisions or rhythmic patterns (figures) are linked to an underlying pulse (ground) or metric system (Bruscia, 1987). Intramusical examples include one player keeping a pulse with one hand and subdividing or improvising figures with the other (as with a piano accompaniment in the left hand and an improvised melody in the right), or that same player maintaining an implied or *internal pulse* while creating subdivisions or rhythmic patterns. Intermusical examples include one or more players keeping a pulse and others creating subdivisions or patterns, as described in the beginning of the vignette. Using the Integration profile, and with an intermusical orientation, you could listen to and describe how each of the figures created by the patients fit with Bob's established ground. To what degree did the durations of sound in each figure coincide with the pulse? Chris's playing was described as "slightly misaligned." What about the others? Were patient responses perfectly aligned, not aligned at all, or somewhere in the middle, coinciding with the ground about half of the time?

Tonal figure-ground relationships have to do with melodic and harmonic elements—specifically, the degree to which improvised melody and harmony is grounded in a scale or key center (Bruscia, 1987). There were no tonal elements present in the above example.

When there are multiple parts sounding simultaneously as in group improvisation, you can use the Integration profile to determine the nature of rhythmic, tonal, and textural *part-whole* relationships in addition to figure-ground relationships (Bruscia, 1987). Each of the individual rhythmic patterns created by the patients of Unit Five would be considered parts and the composite of all patterns would be considered the whole. To what extent did each part correspond with the other parts and with the rhythmic whole? In the case of tonal improvisation, do the lines function to create monophony, homophony, or polyphony?

Textural part-whole relationships relate to role functions. Back to our example: How did each of the players' creations function relative to the overall "fabric" of the piece? Were there several separate grounds, several separate figures, one ground and several figures, etc.?

Gradients in the Integration profile range from "Undifferentiated" (merged, where the figure is the ground or the part is the whole) to

"Overdifferentiated" (where the parts are highly contrasted and incompatible).

Additional Example: The therapist maintains a constant beat on the frame drum. At first, the clients join in with this pulse, playing in identical fashion. At this point, the level of rhythmic integration between the therapist's music and that of the clients would likely be considered "undifferentiated" in that the ground (therapist's playing) and the figures (clients' playing) are one and the same. As many of the clients begin to create simple subdivided rhythmic patterns that line up with the therapist's pulse and tempo, the level of rhythmic integration (again, with the therapist's playing in this case) would move toward "fused" or "integrated." After two or three minutes of improvising, some of these players begin to fall away from the established pulse. Eventually, all but one of the players' rhythmic patterns are totally misaligned with the therapist's playing and that of the other group members. At this point in time, the rhythmic integration would be considered "differentiated" or "overdifferentiated," this classification, again, representing the relationship between the therapist's steady beat and the other players' music. Listening from the perspective of the majority of players, however, the rhythmic integration may be classified differently, depending upon the degree of rhythmic coincidence between the simultaneously sounding parts. (intermusical)

Ex 8–4: Integration (Experiential Learning)

Divide the group in half. One half will improvise on a mix of percussion and tonal instruments. The other half will listen. Designate some listeners to focus on rhythmic integration between the parts and some to focus on tonal integration between the parts. Use the gradients for the Integration profile and support your descriptions with specific examples. Switch roles. Repeat several times.

VARIABILITY. *Competencies addressed in this section include the ability to:*

LI 5   Define Variability.

LI 6   Determine levels of variability in rhythmic, tonal, textural, dynamic, and timbral elements.

Whereas *Integration* refers to vertical features of the music, *Variability* refers to horizontal features, and can be defined as the degree to which something has the ability "to be changed or adapted" (*The New Oxford American Dictionary*, 2001, p. 1870). This profile is used to determine the relationship between sequential aspects of the music, that is, change (or lack of change) over time (Bruscia, 1987). As stated above, at one end, the gradient is "Rigid" (characterized by persistent maintenance or repetition of musical ideas with no changes); on the opposite end of the continuum, the playing would be considered "Random" (with severe and frequent changes that appear to have no meaning). In the above vignette, were there incidents of notable intramusical variability? That is, did any one individual's playing stand out as highly rigid or highly random? What about intermusical variability? Were there aspects of the total group improvisation that remained curiously unchanged? Were there aspects that changed abruptly and without warning? Or was there a balance of sameness and change over time?

<u>*Additional Example:*</u> *As the therapist and three group members gather in the music therapy clinic, they each pick up a different instrument and begin to play. The therapist moves to the conga drum and establishes duple meter with simple accented rhythm patterns. Immediately, two of the three players switch instruments; one of them switches again within a matter of seconds. The third player adds an instrument to the one he has been playing and continues to improvise on the two simultaneously. The second player switches instruments abruptly, and the third player returns to her original instrument until the end of the piece. The therapist remains on the conga. In this scenario, the therapist's purposeful use of timbre (as produced by the specific musical instrument used) would be considered "stable" in that there were no changes. In contrast, the timbral variability of the other players would be considered "contrasting" or "random" in that there were frequent changes, a seeming lack of focus and stability, and resulting fragmentation in the musical product. (intramusical)*

Ex 8–5: Variability (Experiential Learning)

As in the previous exercise, divide the group in half. One half will improvise on a mix of percussion and tonal instruments. The other half will serve as listeners, attending to either rhythmic, tonal, textural, dynamic, or timbral variability over the course of the piece. Use the gradients for Variability and support your descriptions with specific examples. Switch roles. Repeat several times.

TENSION. *Competencies addressed in this section include the ability to:*

LI 7   Define Tension
LI 8   Determine levels of tension in rhythmic, tonal, textural, dynamic, and timbral elements.

The fourth profile is labeled *Tension*. Tension refers to "a strained state or conditions resulting from forces acting in opposition to each other" (*The New Oxford American Dictionary*, 2001, pp. 1748–1749). In an improvisational context, this profile relates the degree of rhythmic, tonal, or expressive tension present in the piece, as perceived by the listener (Bruscia, 1987). On one end, the music is "Hypotense" (with insufficient energy to create tension); on the other, it is "Hypertense" (with unrelenting and overpowering tension). As the student in the vignette, you began to sense tension when the rhythmic ground ceased and the sounds of the various players became "out of sync" with one another; in other words, you sensed intermusical tension. Bruscia (1987) notes that tension is often related to a lack of rhythmic integration, which can occur in solo, dyadic, and group improvisation. How would you classify the level of tension at this point? What about the level of timbral tension when the patient entered with the grating sound of the guiro?

Additional Example: As the group improvises, one of the clients breaks from the pulse and begins playing an unmetered tremolo on the alto metallophone. Other players follow his lead; the group "rumbles" collectively, increasing the volume gradually. One of the players strikes the gong forcefully and all players stop. After a brief period of silence, someone begins a tremolo on the conga drum and the crescendo-gong sequence is repeated. The tension of this excerpt would be considered "cyclic" in that energy was alternately accumulated and released by the entire group. (intermusical)

Ex 8–6: Tension (Experiential Learning)

As in the previous exercise, divide the group in half. One half will improvise on a mix of percussion and tonal instruments. The other half will serve as listeners, attending to and describing the degree of tension in the piece. Use the gradients for Tension and support your descriptions with specific examples. Switch roles. Repeat several times.

CONGRUENCE. *Competencies addressed in this section include the ability to:*

LI 9   *Define Congruence*
LI 10   *Determine levels of congruence between musical elements and physical, programmatic, verbal, and interpersonal features.*

The next profile is called *Congruence.* This profile is used to describe the degree to which various elements are "in agreement and harmony" (*The New Oxford American Dictionary*, 2001, p. 363), here, with levels of tension (feeling states) and role relationships in the other elements. Especially helpful in this profile are the body, program, verbal, and interpersonal scales. All of these are included as a way to reflect the level of consistency between the overall character of the music and tension in the relevant area: the client's body (posture, movements, facial expressions, etc.); the program (lyrics, images, stories, etc.); client verbalizations (reactions to the improvisation); and role relationships (the players' musical and nonmusical connections with one another) (Bruscia, 1987). The continuum for congruence ranges from "Uncommitted" (the element is neutral or indiscernible) to "Polarized" (the element stands out as contradictory to the level of tension in the improvisation as a whole).

Let us return to Karen. Her playing ("lively but barely audible") and her appearance ("disinterested in the entire experience") were at odds. In this case, there was an obvious discrepancy between what she was playing and how her face and posture appeared as she was playing it. Quite simply, her animated sounds did not match her disinterested demeanor. How would you classify this intramusical incongruence? Was the lively nature of her playing congruent with some features but not others? Or was it completely discrepant?

Were there examples of intermusical congruence or incongruence? What about the facial expressions of the players involved in the "copy game"?

Additional Example: A group of music students improvise together on the self-selected referent "anger." Many of the players have angry, scowling expressions on their faces, yet their playing is soft with a thin texture and a noticeable lack of rhythmic or melodic tension. After the improvisation, some of the students discuss how satisfying it was to "express their bitterness and frustration." The level of congruence in this improvisation would probably be considered "polarized" in that the low level of tension afforded by the musical elements (volume, texture, etc.) stands in stark contrast to the referent, facial expressions, and verbalizations of the players. (intramusical and intermusical)

Ex 8–7: Congruence (Experiential Learning)

As in the previous exercise, divide the group in half. One half will improvise on a mix of percussion and tonal instruments. The other half will listen, attending to and describing the degree of congruence between musical elements and the overall feeling state of the piece. Use the gradients for Congruence and support your descriptions with specific examples. Switch roles. Repeat several times.

AUTONOMY. Competencies addressed in this section include the ability to:

LI 11   Define Autonomy

*LI 12   Determine levels of autonomy with respect to rhythmic, tonal,
textural, dynamic, and timbral elements.*

One of the most important profiles in group improvisation is the
Autonomy profile. Autonomy refers to "freedom from external control or
influence" (*The New Oxford American Dictionary*, 2001, p. 109). In an
improvisational context, it represents the degree to which the therapist
and players assume the roles of leader and follower (Bruscia, 1987). As
such, this profile relates only to the intermusical relationships formed
during the improvisation. Gradients in the Autonomy profile range from
"Dependent" (depicting a player who never leads and always follows) to
"Resister" (depicting a player who continually refuses to follow the
leader by ignoring, withdrawing from, or aggressing toward them).

As the student music therapist, you noticed that there was rhythmic
imitation occurring between at least three different patients. Which
player was leading, and is this a consistent role that she or he has
assumed? Which player was following, and is this a consistent role that
she or he has assumed? Or was there a balance in leadership and
followship between these three players?

Additional Example: *During a lengthy tonal group improvisation, the
clients settle into duple meter, playing simple subdivided melodies based
on a consistent implied pulse. Two minutes into the piece, one of the two
therapists in the group begins accenting every third beat in an attempt to
establish triple meter. The co-therapist quickly joins in with the new
meter, but despite the persistent exaggeration of a new downbeat, all of
the other players remain in duple meter for the duration of the
improvisation. According to the Autonomy profile, the clients would be
considered "resisters" in that they continued to control the stability of
the metric aspect of the improvisation, in spite of the therapists' attempts
to entice them to follow. (intermusical)*

Ex 8–8: Autonomy (Experiential Learning)

*As in the previous exercise, divide the group in half. One half will
improvise on a mix of percussion and tonal instruments. The other half*

will serve as listeners, attending to and describing the leadership relationships in the group. Use the gradients for Autonomy and support your descriptions with specific examples. Switch roles. Repeat several times.

SUMMARY AND CAVEATS

Music therapists need some kind of system for managing the in-the-moment listening challenges that are inherent to group improvisation. Without some kind of listening framework and without a consistent vocabulary and nomenclature for description, the actions and materials resulting from group improvisation can be overwhelming and meaningless. One system for listening is called the Improvisation Assessment Profiles (IAPs). The IAPs are composed of six profiles, each of which centers on a specific musical process. These profiles help us understand and classify the musical relationships that individual and multiple players create during improvisation. In this chapter, each of the profiles has been described and linked to clinical examples.

It is critical that you remember that the IAPs were originally designed as an assessment tool for use by professionals. In other words, it is not responsible to use the profiles to make determinations about client diagnosis or treatment goals without proper training. And, like any valid assessment tool, the IAPs are intended to be used in conjunction with other relevant information as gained from the client's personal and clinical history (Bruscia, 1987).

You must also understand that the IAPs, both as assessment tools and as in-the-moment listening guides, are designed to help us recognize *tendencies* in a client's musical improvisations *over time* (Bruscia, 1987). In other words, it is neither accurate nor fair to assume on the basis of your single observation of the patients of Unit Five that the player whose syncopated rhythmic patterns were misaligned with the pulse is resistant to playing "in sync" with other group members or that he has a motor planning problem that prevents him from doing so. While both of these are valid possibilities, you can not know for sure what is happening until you gather more relevant information and witness musical tendencies over time.

Vocabulary for Chapter Eight

1. *Musical Elements*
2. *Intramusical*
3. *Intermusical*
4. *Salience*
5. *Integration*
6. *Variability*
7. *Tension*
8. *Congruence*
9. *Autonomy*
10. *Gradients*
11. *Listening Set*
12. *Figure-Ground*
13. *Internal Pulse*
14. *Part-Whole*

Chapter Nine

VERBAL PROCESSING

Chapters One through Eight have had as their focus those skills used *before* and *during* improvisation. Let us now turn our attention to the kinds of things that you may need to do *after* the music-making. The first thing you will need to decide is if the improvisation experience will be processed in any way.

To Process or Not to Process

Sometimes improvisation experiences are followed by focused discussion, or what is commonly called *verbal processing*. You probably already know that not all models of clinical music improvisation involve verbal processing, and even among those that do, not all experiences or sessions are necessarily discussed. Improvisation can be processed through other modalities, such as mandala art, movement, writing, role playing, etc. However, the skillful use of these modalities requires advanced training, in my opinion, whereas entry-level facilitators can learn to effectively and ethically use certain verbal techniques and, in fact, are expected to do so in accordance with the AMTA *Professional Competencies*. Of course, if your clients do not have the ability to communicate verbally or through alternative means, such as sign language or the use of computers, this issue is neither here nor there. If your clients are verbal, however, you will need to decide at some point if verbal processing is warranted. I say "at some point" because the decision may be made before you even meet the clients and play together, or it may be made in the spur of the moment in response to immediate observations or intuitions. In certain well-functioning, mature groups, the clients themselves may be able to determine whether or not it will be beneficial to talk about what has occurred.

One of the factors that may influence this decision ahead of the mark is the therapist's philosophy about the role of music in health and treatment. For example, if you operate from the philosophical perspective that the musical processes and products stemming from improvisation are transformative in and of themselves—this can be referred to as music *as* therapy (Bruscia, 1987, 1995)—there may be no need to talk about what has occurred. If, on the other hand, you believe that discussing what has happened is a prerequisite for insight or for the consolidation of learning—music *in* therapy (Bruscia, 1987, 1995)—then verbal processing will most certainly be an indispensable feature of the entire process.

Decisions about verbal processing are also linked to therapeutic aim in that sometimes what you intend to accomplish may only be achieved and/or demonstrated through group discussion. That is, if an established group goal is to be more forthcoming verbally about improvisation experiences, then discourse is an inevitability.

In addition to philosophical orientation and therapeutic aim, there are other factors that influence the decision of whether or not to verbally process improvisation. In fact, at each stage of treatment—assessment, treatment, evaluation, and termination—there may be advantages to processing. During *assessment*, verbal processing can help you gather important information about the cognitive, emotional, and communicative functioning of the clients. For instance, if a client offers a jumbled account of the series of musical events during a brief improvisation (e.g., who started, what happened in the middle, what happened at the end?), he may be revealing memory or perceptual deficits that would otherwise be unapparent. Or, if a client has trouble describing her intrapersonal experience without crying profusely every time she attempts, she may be revealing emotional fragility. And verbal discourse may quickly expose or lend support to musical manifestations of various roles and relationships within the group, sometimes termed *group dynamics*.

During *treatment*, conversation about the experiences of the clients can serve to strengthen rapport as the group moves through various stages of development (Yalom, 1995). When one member shares her thoughts and feelings, understanding and compassion can grow; when these offerings are verbally accepted and validated by the therapist and the other members, trust deepens within the group. Thoughts, feelings, and opinions that are shared during a session can also help the therapist determine the best course of action within the session; in other words, what a client talks about in response to an experience can help you make in-the-moment treatment decisions about what comes next.

Periodic, focused discussion about improvisation processes and products can assist you in your *evaluation* of whether specific goals and objectives are being met. For instance, you may be able to track progress among clients who have expressive aphasia by noting their ability over time to label objects and reactions related to the improvisations.

Finally, verbal processing can help you and your clients work through some of the tasks related to termination, most notably the expression and exploration of feelings about ending therapy and the making of a healthy separation (McGuire & Smeltekop, 1994).

There may be times when verbal processing is contraindicated because it is counterproductive to therapy. For example, certain clients may repeatedly use words to berate, exploit, or wound themselves or others; other clients may use verbalization as an intellectual defense against the exploration of emotional conflict and pain.

Focal Point of Verbal Processing

Once the therapist (or clients) decide to engage in verbal discourse, it is usually helpful to determine a focus for the discussion. Again, this can be established ahead of time or in the moment. Let me reiterate that nearly every decision you make as a therapist revolves around your clinical intentions! So, if you have made sound choices *before* and *during* the improvisation, the processing *after* the music-making ought to follow naturally from these decisions.

Consider for a moment that for any group improvisation experience or session there are at least four overarching foci for discourse, these being created by the interface between what happens within the music or outside of the music and what happens within a single player or between multiple players. As defined elsewhere in this text, these connections are called *intramusical, intermusical, intrapersonal,* and *interpersonal.* Read the following clinical vignette, which should help illustrate this point.

Vignette 9–1

You are working with a group of four hospitalized adults with mental disorders, and your aim is to provide opportunities for and aid the clients' efforts to make meaningful and empathic connections with one another. You have carefully chosen procedural and relationship givens for the experience: One at a time, each of the players selects an instrument of her or his choice and begins to play some aspect of self that she or he wishes to reveal to the group (a mood, an attribute, etc.). The other players listen carefully and gradually join in the improvisation, reflecting as closely as they can the character of the soloist's playing. After each improvisation, you facilitate a conversation about the experience. To start the flow, you might use a general, open-ended probe directed at the solo player, such as, "Talk about that experience." More specifically, you might ask her or him "What feelings do/did you have about your own playing?" (intrapersonal), "How did the tempo of your playing relate to your changes in meter?" (intramusical), "How well did the group members reflect the character of your improvisation?" (interpersonal), or "How did the group's tempo fit with your own?" (intermusical).

Role of the Therapist

Your level of involvement in the verbal processing of improvisation can be conceptualized as a continuum: On one end you might be completely *nondirective*, contributing to the conversation as an equal member of the group without guiding the content or process; on the other end you might be completely *directive*, determining the focus of discourse, the length of the processing session, and even the order in which group members speak. Often, the role that you assume during the processing will be consistent with the role you assumed during the music-making, but not always.

The depth of discussion can be related to your role as a therapist. With nondirective leadership, clients could be allowed to discuss whatever they choose, and casual comments such as "That was great, I thoroughly enjoyed myself!" or "That did not turn out the way I had anticipated!" would be taken at face value and left unexplored unless another client was inclined to investigate them more fully. With directive leadership, the specific focus could be determined for the clients, superficial comments might be explored more fully, and all clients would be encouraged to examine their inner experiences (intrapersonal) as well as their experiences with others (interpersonal). The interpretation of meaning from a particular theoretical orientation (e.g., psychodynamic, cognitive, etc.) may enter the process when the therapist takes a directive approach.

Be aware, however, that nondirective leadership does not necessarily imply superficiality; in certain groups, clients can explore issues at a meaningful level without the therapist's continuous assistance. Nor does directive leadership necessarily imply depth; it is possible for a leader to assert her or his decisive authority without delving into meaningful or fruitful verbal processing!

Verbal Techniques

Many authors have written about the kinds of verbal techniques that are useful in helping others to disclose their perceptions, thoughts, feelings, ideas, values, and opinions (Bruscia, 1987; Corey et al., 2004; Meier & Davis, 2001; Okun, 2001). I find that I rely most heavily upon eight distinct verbal techniques as I process improvisation experiences. These are probe, paraphrase, reflection of feeling, clarification, checking out, confrontation, self-disclosure, and summary. My undergraduate students are encouraged to practice using six of these: probe, reflection of feeling, clarification, checking out, minimal self-disclosure, and summary. Although not a comprehensive list, in my opinion, these six techniques provide the beginning facilitator of improvisation most of what she or he needs in order to guide effective and ethical discourse about improvisation experiences.

Competencies addressed herein include the following:

VP 1   *Use probes to elicit client conversation about group improvisation experiences.*

VP 2	*Use reflection of feeling to demonstrate empathy for the clients.*
VP 3	*Use clarification to elucidate the clients' group improvisation experiences.*
VP 4	*Use checking out to respond to intuition.*
VP 5	*Use self-disclosure to build and strengthen intimacy with clients.*
VP 6	*Use summary to close the improvisation experience or session.*

In this section of the chapter, I will define each technique, give at least one example, and, as appropriate, provide an exercise for dyadic or group practice. Before we move to the specific techniques, however, let us take a look at Barbara Okun's general guidelines for the use of verbal techniques (2001, p. 82):

1. Phrase your response in the same vocabulary that the [client] uses.
2. Speak slowly enough that the [client] understands each word.
3. Use concise rather than rambling statements.
4. Relate the topic introduced by the client to the identified cognitive theme that is of the most importance.
5. Talk directly to the client, not about him or her.
6. Send "I" statements to "own" your feelings, and allow the client to reject, accept, or modify your messages.
7. Encourage the client to talk about his or her feelings.
8. Time your responses to facilitate, not block, communication.

Probe

The *probe* is used to elicit a descriptive and sometimes detailed verbal response from the players. Although often phrased as a question (e.g., "What were your reactions to the very end of the improvisation?"), probes also take the form of statements with stems such as "Tell us more about your reactions to. ..." or "Share your impression of ..." Notice that probes, whether delivered as a question or a directive, are phrased in an *open-ended* way so that the players feel invited to share description and detail. *Closed-ended* probes are those questions that result in a simple "yes" or "no" response. Closed-ended questions are valuable in their own right, but not as a means of stimulating verbalization. A string of closed-ended queries can either result in the players feeling barraged or bring the verbal sharing to a screeching halt. In general, then, try not to begin probes with phrases like "Did you. ...?," "Were you. ...?," and "Have you. ...?," and instead use questions that start with "How did you. ...?," "Why were you. ...?," and "When have you ...?" (I sometimes caution my students about the use of "Why" in that it can be perceived by some individuals as having an accusatory tone.)

When music is created in a spontaneous way as in improvisation, themes or salient issues may emerge and evolve as the music unfolds; dialogue is necessarily more immediate and dynamic than that used to process other, more predictable music therapy experiences (Gardstrom, 2001). The possibilities for discussion are thus vast, and you will often be called upon to think "on your feet" and talk "off the cuff," a style of facilitation that many people find intimidating. Below are a few generic "conversation starters" (probes) that have proven helpful in my work with verbal adolescents and adults. They must be adapted to fit the individualized needs of client groups and the situation at hand. (Note that some of these probes are process oriented and some are product oriented. Note also that both musical and personal relationships are represented.)

1. Talk about that, please.
2. What was that like for you?
3. What would you like to say about that?
4. What did you hear in/notice about your own or others' music?
5. What did you like/dislike about that?
6. How immersed were you in your own music-making?
7. What surprises (pleasant or unpleasant) did you encounter?
8. How satisfied do you feel?
9. What thoughts ran through your mind during the improvisation?
10. What emotions did you experience during the improvisation?

11. What images, memories, or associations did the experience evoke?
12. In general, what was the nature of your connection with the other players?

Ex 9–1 (Experiential Learning)

Improvise together. Take turns suggesting probes that might be appropriate for eliciting conversation about various aspects of the experience.

Reflection of Feeling

Reflection of feeling is another technique of empathy. In Chapter Seven, we learned that reflection is the term used to describe a musical facilitation technique whose "aim is to match the underlying *emotional character* of the clients' actions" in order to convey understanding. In reflection of feeling, the therapist represents (with content and expressive demeanor) the underlying emotional character of the client's words. Take a look at Appendix C. We used this list of emotions previously to guide our exploration of referential improvisation. Now the list can serve as an *emotional vocabulary list* as you practice reflecting feelings of others in the group. (A helpful list of categorized feeling words can also be found in Borczon, *Music Therapy: A Fieldwork Primer*, 2004, pp. 64–65.)

The initial example (frantic playing in the group) can be used here to illustrate how probe and reflection of feeling can work together to invite meaningful conversation:

Client: I wish we hadn't played in such a frantic manner.
Therapist (probe): What about that seemed frantic?
Client: The way we were all playing different rhythms without any common beat at the very end. It felt chaotic and undone! And now I feel nervous.
Therapist (reflection of feeling): The turmoil at the end was nerve-racking for you.
Client: Yeah. My hands are sweating …
Therapist (probe): What was it like for the rest of you?

Ex 9–2 (Experiential Learning)

Improvise together. Take turns leading a discussion that uses reflection of feeling to elicit verbal sharing and convey empathy.

Clarification

Clarification is one of the simplest verbal techniques that a therapist can use; the challenge comes in knowing when to use it. The purposes of *clarification* are to clear up confusion or, more simply, to be sure that you have heard and correctly understood what the client is attempting to communicate. The most common way to clarify is to use an approach such as "I want to be sure that I understand you. Are you saying that …?" In the grand scheme of things, it is not terribly important to always be "on the mark"; even if you have misunderstood what the client was trying to say, the clarification serves to convey your interest in the client, as well as your commitment to her or his treatment. In this way, the technique of clarification can serve not only to enhance communication, but to strengthen rapport.

Client: I wish I had taken a more active lead in the improvisation. Instead, I depended on others to set the pace, change the loudness, and all of that.
Therapist (probe): How does that compare with what you usually do?
Client: Usually I have more of a voice. I don't know, but for some reason today I had absolutely no drive, no motivation to connect with anyone in the music. I just wanted to blend in to the total sound and let everyone else determine what was supposed to happen. It's weird. I feel like my mom must have felt right after my dad died.
Therapist (clarification): Let me see if I understand you. Are you saying that your mom lost her will to connect with others after your dad passed away?
Client: I'm saying that she became meek and dependent, even clingy. I don't want to be like that …

Ex 9–3 (Experiential Learning)

Improvise together. Take turns leading a discussion, using clarification as appropriate.

Checking Out

Checking out is often mistaken for clarification. Whereas clarification involves responding to something that has been said outright by the client, checking out involves responding to a therapist's internal hunch about what has been said or, in some cases, what has not been said. A hunch, or intuition, may result from any number of nonverbal cues as well, including the client's posture, gestures, and facial affect. Here again, it is important to recognize that the line between checking out and interpretation can be quite thin.

Common stems for checking out include "I have a hunch that …," "I get the sense that …," "I wonder if …," and "It seems to me as though …" Here is an example of how checking out may be used in dialogue:

Client: He played the cabasa without stopping for about five minutes, on and on …
Therapist (probe): What was your response to that?
Client: I wondered why he did that. He did the same thing last time. Some of the members of the group even told him that they didn't like the harsh sound of the instrument.
Therapist (checking out): It seems to me that you are irritated with him. Are you?
Client: Well, yeah, I guess I am. It's just that he always talks over other people and acts like what he has to say is more important than anyone else's opinion.
Therapist (checking out): I wonder if there's another reason that you are irritated with him …?
Client: I suppose.

Ex 9–4 (Experiential Learning)

Improvise together. Take turns leading a discussion, using checking out to confirm hunches as appropriate.

Self-Disclosure

Self-disclosure is a technique whose function is to "enhance the helping relationship and aid in problem solving" (Okun, 2001, p. 287). In self-disclosure, the therapist shares personal information with the client. Obviously, the technique must be used discreetly and always for the client's rather than the therapist's advantage. An example of effective and ethical self-disclosure follows:

<u>Client:</u> As we listened to the recording of the improvisation, I could actually hear the frustration and sadness in my playing. It was a reminder of how much unhappiness I feel when I am with her.
<u>Therapist</u> (reflection of feeling): ... of how much sadness you feel in the relationship ...
<u>Client:</u> Yes. And even though I'm so miserable, I am scared to death to make any kind of change. I just feel stuck in my own fear. It was all there in the music. *(Crying)* I know I need to get out, but I just can't seem to find the courage to take the first step.
<u>Therapist</u> (self-disclosure): It's difficult, I know. When I am afraid, I have a hard time seeing beyond the horror to what that first positive step could be.

Summary

A *summary* serves four main functions in a clinical session. First, it affords the therapist an opportunity to highlight the sequential action taken during the session. Second, it allows the therapist to identify the main themes to have emerged. Third, the summary provides an opportunity for the clients to discuss their final reactions to the session. Finally, the summary is an appropriate time to look ahead to the next session and, perhaps, make some decisions about what will occur or what goals will be addressed. Summaries can range in length from brief (three to four sentences) to lengthy (three to four minutes), depending on the situation and the clients' needs.

Here is an example of a summary from a 45-minute session with a group of adults with chronic mental illness living in a hospital:

Therapist (summary): Today we began with a brief warm-up on the drums. Then we progressed to an improvisation on the group of emotions that we often label "sadness." Many of you talked openly about how your lives in the hospital are defined by loneliness and, in particular, about the anger and hopelessness that you feel when you realize that you have been abandoned by your family and friends. Does anyone have any further reactions to share? (patients talk) We discussed the need to find and cling to hope, and we talked about the possibility of writing a song about hope during our next session together. How does that sound to everyone?

Vocabulary for Chapter Nine

1. *Verbal Processing*
2. *Group Dynamics*
3. *Nondirective*
4. *Directive*
5. *Probe*
6. *Reflection of Feeling*
7. *Clarification*
8. *Checking Out*
9. *Self-Disclosure*
10. *Summary*

Chapter Ten

CLOSING

The primary purpose of this book has been to address, in a systematic way, each of the improvisation competencies that I have asserted are critical for the effective and ethical facilitation of clinical music improvisation with client groups. These competencies have been presented in a sequential manner, beginning with those skills that are typically needed and used *before* improvisation, the Preparatory Skills. I would like to stress the importance of this particular skill set, in that what you do beforehand can have a profound effect on the overall success of the improvisation experience. The more prepared you are before the clients appear for music therapy, the more confident and relaxed you are likely to be when the actual facilitation begins. With a self-assured and relaxed demeanor, you can orient your primary focus toward the clients' needs rather than your own and respond to intuitions as you move through the process.

From Preparatory Skills, we moved to those skills that are needed and used *during* improvisation, namely the Nonmusical and Musical Facilitation techniques and Listening Skills. Using your body, gestures, words, music, and ears in a meaningful way to enrich the clients' immediate experiences was the focus of these particular competencies.

We concluded with those skills that are needed and used *after* improvisation, when the music has ceased. Your toolbox must include Verbal Techniques such as probe, paraphrase, reflection of feeling, etc., in order for you to facilitate conversation about improvisation processes and products and thereby help verbal clients articulate and integrate the significant aspects of their experience, gain new insights and develop connections with others.

Undoubtedly, you encountered some challenges along each step of the way. I hope that you were able to overcome some of those challenges through practice, discussion, and reflection. Take a moment now to respond to the following series of exercises as a way to take stock of your progress, current status, and future focus.

Ex 10–1 (Ind/Exp)

Take a moment to reflect (out loud or on paper) on the following questions. You may choose to seek feedback from others about your own skill development in this area. Of the numerous Preparatory Skills (*see* Appendix A):

1. Which two or three skills were the easiest for me to develop?
2. Which two or three skills were the most difficult for me to develop?
3. What specific steps can I take to continue to develop my competency in these difficult areas?

Ex 10–2 (Ind/Exp)

Take a moment to reflect (out loud or on paper) on the following questions. You may choose to seek feedback from others about your own skill development in this area. Of the Nonmusical Facilitation Skills (*see* Appendix A):

1. Which two or three skills were the easiest for me to develop?
2. Which two or three skills were the most difficult for me to develop?
3. What specific steps can I take to continue to develop my competency in these difficult areas?

Ex 10–3 (Ind/Exp)

Take a moment to reflect (out loud or on paper) on the following questions. You may choose to seek feedback from others about your own skill development in this area. Of the Musical Facilitation Skills (*see* Appendix A):

1. Which two or three skills were the easiest for me to develop?
2. Which two or three skills were the most difficult for me to develop?
3. What specific steps can I take to continue to develop my competency in these difficult areas?

Ex 10–4 (Ind/Exp)

Take a moment to reflect (out loud or on paper) on the following questions. You may choose to seek feedback from others about your own skill development in this area. Of the Listening Skills (*see* Appendix A):
1. Which two or three skills were the easiest for me to develop?
2. Which two or three skills were the most difficult for me to develop?
3. What specific steps can I take to continue to develop my competency in these difficult areas?

Ex 10–5 (Ind/Exp)

Take a moment to reflect (out loud or on paper) on the following questions. You may choose to seek feedback from others about your own skill development in this area. Of the Verbal Skills (*see* Appendix A):
1. Which two or three skills were the easiest for me to develop?
2. Which two or three skills were the most difficult for me to develop?
3. What specific steps can I take to continue to develop my competency in these difficult areas?

In the introductory chapter of this book, I wrote that

> music therapists who have developed clinical music skills are able to create music in an authentic, communicative, flexible, and intentional manner. In this context, *authentic* means with genuineness of expression, *communicative* means with a desire and ability to make meaningful contact with the other players, *flexible* means in a responsive and adaptable manner, and *intentional* means with a clear clinical purpose in mind. It is, perhaps, a combination of these four dimensions that therapists ultimately ought to strive to achieve in their improvisational work.

With respect to these notions, I would like to encourage you to consider your personal perspective on how evaluations of beauty and meaning are made with respect to improvisational products. Some individuals believe that an improvisation is "beautiful" or "meaningful" if and only if it demonstrates internal structure, technical sophistication, expressive fluency, broad or lasting allure, and so forth—criteria often employed in conventional musical aesthetics. Others believe that an improvisation can be "beautiful" or "meaningful" by virtue of the players' sincerity of expression or fidelity to the task or referent, even though the piece itself may not be technically complex, eloquent, or even appealing to the listeners. With this second perspective, I come full circle to the importance of authentic and clinically relevant musical self-expression; here, one's ability to create and facilitate beautiful and meaningful improvisations is integrally linked to one's own ability to play in a genuine and intentional manner.

In closing, I hope that the information presented in this text combined with your diligence as a learner has helped you to become more genuine, communicative, and adaptable in your own group improvisation. As you continue to develop these features and combine them with clinical intentionality, you will be able to effectively lead your clients to and through the journey and joy of clinical music improvisation.

Appendix A
Essential Competencies for Clinical Improvisation

<u>Preparatory Skills (PR)</u>

___PR 1	*Define clinical music improvisation.*
___PR 2	*Define and accurately use terms relevant to clinical music improvisation (e.g., method, technique, referential, nonreferential, etc.)*
___PR 3	*Identify by name all instruments in the improvisation instrumentarium.*
___PR 4	*Select instruments for the improvisation experience based upon knowledge and perception of the players' attributes, needs, and clinical objectives.*
___PR 5	*Arrange the improvisation environment with attention to the relative positioning of the instruments, the players, and the leader.*
___PR 6	*Present/introduce the instruments to the players in a manner that enables their effective use.*
___PR 7	*Identify the rhythmic elements commonly used in clinical improvisation.*
___PR 8	*Establish and maintain pulse in a variety of tempi.*
___PR 9	*Establish and maintain subdivisions of the pulse.*
___PR 10	*Establish duple and triple meters with the use of dynamic accents.*
___PR 11	*Create simple and complex rhythmic patterns in duple and triple meters.*
___PR 12	*Create effective rhythmic flourishes.*
___PR 13	*Identify the tonal elements commonly used in clinical improvisation.*
___PR 14	*Create melodies in a variety of modalities and tonalities.*
___PR 15	*Improvise simple harmonic structures.*
___PR 16	*Memorize and reproduce several harmonic vamps.*
___PR 17	*Identify the textural elements commonly used in clinical improvisation.*
___PR 18	*Assume a variety of musical roles to create a variety of textures.*

___PR 19 *Demonstrate multiple playing configurations on each instrument.*

___PR 20 *Identify the dynamic elements commonly used in clinical improvisation.*

___PR 21 *Create gradual and sudden changes in volume.*

___PR 22 *Identify the timbral elements commonly used in clinical improvisation.*

___PR 23 *Demonstrate multiple timbres on each instrument.*

___PR 24 *Identify suitable structures for improvisation sessions.*

___PR 25 *Determine and present suitable givens and referents for improvisation experiences.*

Facilitative Skills (Nonmusical/NM)

___NM 1 *Start and stop the improvisation if necessary.*

___NM 2 *Communicate with players nonverbally while improvising.*

___NM 3 *Communicate with players verbally while improvising.*

___NM 4 *Move within and around the group while improvising for purposes of support or guidance.*

___NM 5 *Help the players produce sound on the percussion instruments as necessary (e.g., position the instrument, hold the instrument, provide hand-over-hand assistance).*

Facilitative Skills (Musical/MU)

___MU 1 *Imitate a client's response.*

___MU 2 *Synchronize with a client's playing.*

___MU 3 *Incorporate a musical motif of the client into one's improvising.*

___MU 4 *Pace one's improvising with the client's energy level.*

___MU 5 *Reflect the moods, attitudes, and feelings exhibited by the client.*

___MU 6 *Establish and maintain a rhythmic ground.*

___MU 7 *Establish and maintain a tonal center.*

___MU 8 *Use repetition as an invitation for the client to respond.*

___MU 9 *Model desired musical responses.*

___*MU 10*   *Make spaces in one's improvising for the client's improvising.*

___*MU 11*   *Interject music into the spaces made by the client.*

___*MU 12*   *Introduce musical change to redirect the client's playing.*

___*MU 13*   *Intensify elements within the improvisation.*

___*MU 14*   *Assist clients in the sharing of the instruments.*

___*MU 15*   *Bond with the client through the creation and repetition of a musical theme.*

___*MU 16*   *Demonstrate the effective use of musical soliloquy.*

___*MU 17*   *Recede from playing during a group improvisation.*

___*MU 18*   *Improvise to a client's free association.*

Facilitative Skills (Listening/LI)

___*LI 1*   *Define salience.*

___*LI 2*   *Determine what elements and aspects of improvisation are salient at any given time.*

___*LI 3*   *Define integration.*

___*LI 4*   *Determine levels of integration for rhythmic, tonal, textural, dynamic, and timbral elements.*

___*LI 5*   *Define variability.*

___*LI 6*   *Determine levels of variability in rhythmic, tonal, dynamic, and timbral elements.*

___*LI 7*   *Define tension.*

___*LI 8*   *Determine levels of tension in rhythmic, tonal, textural, dynamic, and timbral elements.*

___*LI 9*   *Define congruence.*

___*LI 10*   *Determine levels of congruence between musical elements and physical, programmatic, verbal, and interpersonal features.*

___*LI 11*   *Define autonomy.*

___*LI 12*   *Determine levels of autonomy with respect to rhythmic, tonal, textural, dynamic, and timbral elements.*

Verbal Processing Skills (VP)

___*VP 1*   *Use probes to elicit client conversation about group improvisation experiences.*

___*VP 2*   *Use reflection of feeling to demonstrate empathy for the clients.*

___*VP 3*   *Use clarification to elucidate the clients' group improvisation experiences.*

___*VP 4*   *Use checking out to respond to intuition.*

___*VP 5*   *Use self-disclosure to build and strengthen intimacy with clients.*

___*VP 6*   *Use summary to close the improvisation experience or session.*

156

Appendix B
Exercises

Did = Didactic Learning
Exp = Experiential Learning
Ind = Independent Skill Development

Chapter Two

2–1 (Exp)	*Improvising static and dynamic referents.* `
	(optional)

Chapter Three

3–1 (Ind)	*Manipulating instruments.*
3–2 (Ind)	*Exploring the timbre of instruments.*
3–3 (Exp)	*Playing and passing instruments in a circle.*
3–4 (Did)	*Sorting the instruments into categories.*
3–5 (Ind)	*Ranking instruments according to strength, etc.*
3–6 (Ind)	*Ranking instruments according to sound variability*
3–7 (Exp)	*Selecting instruments for various populations.*
3–8 (Exp)	*Arranging and rearranging the environment.*
3–9 (Exp)	*Presenting a sound vocabulary.*

Chapter Four

4–1 (Exp)	*Feeling the pulse.*
4–2 (Exp)	*Internalizing the pulse.*
4–3 (Exp)	*Subdividing the pulse.*
4–4 (Exp)	*Using dynamic accents.*
4–5 (Exp)	*Using language to create rhythmic patterns.*
4–6 (Exp)	*Using songs to explore phrasing.*
4–7 (Exp)	*Improvising short rhythmic patterns.*
4–8 (Exp)	*Using binary form to explore rubato playing.*
4–9 (Exp)	*Assuming various rhythmic roles in group playing.*
4–10 (Ind)	*Exploring various scales and modalities.*
4–11 (Ind)	*Improvising tonally with a partner.*
4–12 (Ind)	*Memorizing vamps.*
4–13 (Exp)	*Exploring pitch register and tessitura.*
4–14 (Exp)	*Exploring demands of various role relationships.*

Appendix C
Referents for Clinical Music Improvisation

Static and Dynamic Referents: Emotions
(Note: With children, the words, "mad," "sad," "glad," and "scared" serve as helpful summaries of four main categories of feelings with which they can identify. Under each of these categories below, related terms appear. The final words in each category are slang expressions used to describe the feeling. Because human emotion is subjective, there may be differences of opinion about the category in which a descriptor belongs. Notice that some words appear multiple times; this is an indication of the complexity of human emotion. For example, betrayal may feel like a mixture of anger and sadness. The fifth and sixth categories, "Ambivalent," and "Confused," appear on the following page.)

Mad	"Hopping mad"	Negative	Jolly
Abused	"Fit to be tied"	Neglected	Joyful
Agitated	"Teed off"	Shamed	Lucky
Angry		Somber	Peaceful
Annoyed	**Sad**	Vacant	Positive
Betrayed	Abandoned	"Down in the dumps"	Relieved
Bothered	Anguished	"Down in the mouth"	Satisfied
Cross	Betrayed		Secure
Enraged	Depressed		Thankful
Exasperated	Disappointed	**Glad**	Thrilled
Exploited	Dismal	Blissful	"Pleased as punch"
Horrified	Empty	Carefree	"Happy as a lark"
Humiliated	Forsaken	Certain	
Frustrated	Gloomy	Cheerful	
Furious	Grieving	Comforted	**Scared**
Incensed	Grim	Confident	Abused
Irritated	Heartbroken	Content	Afraid
Irate	Humiliated	Delighted	Agitated
Livid	Isolated	Ecstatic	Alarmed
Perturbed	Lonely	Fortunate	Anxious
Riled	Lost	Gratified	Apprehen-sive
Seething	Miserable	Happy	
Upset			

160

Cowardly	Panicky	Traumatized	"Scared
Edgy	Petrified	Timid	stiff"
Fearful	Shocked	Uneasy	
Fretful	Startled	Worried	
Horrified	Tense	"Worried to	
Nervous	Terrified	death"	

Ambivalent
Cautious
Changeable
Erratic
Fickle
Hesitant
Inconsistent
Indecisive
Irresolute
Tentative
Uncertain
Unpredictable
Unsure
Vacillating
Wavering
"Wishy-washy"

Confused
Baffled
Bamboozled
Befuddled
Bewildered
Confounded
Dazed
Disoriented
Mystified
Overcome
Perplexed
Puzzled
"At a complete loss"
"In a fog"

Static and Dynamic Referents: Events and Processes

1. Birth
2. Birthday Party
3. Breaking Up
4. Circus/Theme Park
5. City Street
6. Dawn
7. Death
8. Divorce
9. Dream
10. Dusk
11. Emotional Abuse
12. Family Meal
13. Fight

14.   Finding Myself/Ourselves
15.   Finishing a Task
16.   Funeral
17.   Getting Drunk
18.   Getting Sick
19.   Giving Up/Quitting
20.   Going for a Walk
21.   Graduation
22.   Growing Old
23.   Holidays
24.   Illness
25.   Imagery
26.   Joining a New Group
27.   Losing Weight
28.   Lovemaking
29.   Marriage
30.   Moving Away
31.   Physical Abuse
32.   Putting on Weight
33.   Rainstorm
34.   Recovery
35.   Relapse
36.   Returning Home
37.   Sexual Abuse
38.   Taking a Trip
39.   Talking to God
40.   Treatment
41.   Typical Day
42.   Verbal Abuse

Static and Dynamic Referents: Interpersonal and Intrapersonal
Relationships

1.   My/Our Mother(s)
2.   My/Our Father(s)
3.   My/Our Sister(s)
4.   My/Our Brother(s)
5.   My/Our Grandmother(s)

6. My/Our Grandfather(s)
7. My/Our Uncle(s)
8. My/Our Aunt(s)
9. My/Our Cousin(s)
10. My/Our Pet(s)
11. My/Our Family/Families
12. My/Our Spouse(s)/Partner(s)
13. My/Our Child/Children
14. My/Our Teacher(s)
15. My/Our Boss(es)
16. My/Our Coworker(s)
17. My/Our Employee(s)
18. My/Our Mentor(s)
19. My/Our Friend(s)
20. My/Our Pastor(s)
21. My/Our God(s)
22. My/Our Doctor(s)
23. My/Our Therapist(s)
24. My/Our Anima (Female)
25. My/Our Animus (Male)
26. My/Our Shadow
27. My/Our Real Self
28. My/Our Ideal Self
29. My/Our Id
30. My/Our Ego
31. My/Our Superego
32. My/Our Group

Static and Dynamic Referents: Expressions and Figures of Speech (Metaphors and Similes)

1. Against the grain
2. All or nothing
3. Back to square one
4. Better safe than sorry
5. Between a rock and a hard place
6. Business as usual
7. Calm before the storm

8.   Can of worms
9.   Dead in the water
10.   Divide and conquer
11.   Dog eat dog
12.   Easy come, easy go
13.   Easy does it
14.   Fight fire with fire
15.   First things first
16.   Home away from home
17.   Left high and dry
18.   Lesser of two evils
19.   Light at the end of the tunnel
20.   Like a dream come true
21.   Like a fish out of water
22.   Marching to a different drummer
23.   Monkey see, monkey do
24.   No way, José
25.   On the sunny side of the street
26.   Once bitten, twice shy
27.   One day at a time
28.   Sink or swim
29.   Survival of the fittest
30.   Up the creek without a paddle

Continuum Referents
(Note: For each of the following, the order may be reversed, depending upon the clinical objective.)

1.   Alone to Together
2.   Anxious to Calm
3.   Anger to Acceptance
4.   Blame to Forgiveness
5.   Confusion to Clarity
6.   Darkness to Light
7.   Death to Immortality
8.   Denial to Acceptance
9.   Fragmentation to Wholeness

164

Appendix D
Harmonic Progressions/Vamps

Major:

1. **I–V(7)**
   (duple or triple meter)

2. **I–IV**
   (duple or triple meter)

3. **I–bVII**
   (duple or triple meter)

4. **I–vi–IV–V(7)**
   ('50's Rock, duple meter)

5. **I–vi–ii–V(7)**
   (*Heart and Soul*, duple meter)

6. **ii–V(7)–I–vi**
   ('40's Swing, duple meter)

7. **I–bII–bIII–bII**
   (Spanish, triple meter)

8. **I–V–vi–iii–IV–I–IV–V(7)**
   (*Canon in D,* duple meter)

9. **I(7)–IV(7)–I(7)–I(7)**
   IV(7)–IV(7)–I(7)–I(7)
   V(7)–IV(7)–I(7)–V(7)
   (12-Bar Blues, duple meter)

Minor:

1. **i–V(7)**
   (duple or triple meter)

2.   **i–v**
     (duple or triple meter)

3.   **i–bVII–bVI–V(7)**
     (*Hit the Road, Jack,* duple meter)

Appendix E
Givens/Parameters

Vocabulary Givens (stipulate *what* takes place)

1. Instruments (only the hand drums are provided for use)

   _____

2. Volume (players are directed to improvise at a *fortissimo* level)

   _____

3. Tempo (the leader begins the improvisation at a very slow tempo
   and does not waver)

   _____

4. Meter (players are instructed to play in 6/8 meter)

   _____

5. Rhythm (players are directed to explore dotted and syncopated
   rhythmic figures throughout the improvisation)

   _____

6. Tonality (the melodic instruments are set up in a Chinese
   pentatonic scale)

   _____

168

7. Harmony (the 12-bar blues is used as the structure for a vocal improvisation)

_____

8. Timbre (only the bell-like instruments are provided for use)

_____

9. Texture (players are instructed to play two instruments simultaneously throughout the improvisation)

_____

10. Referential (players are instructed to play "dawn to dusk")

_____

11. Referential (players are instructed to play "grief")

_____

Procedural Givens (stipulate *when* or *how long* certain events take place)

1. "One person start and the rest of us will join in gradually."

_____

2. "Let's start at *pp* and *crescendo* to the end."

_____

3. "Focus first on your own sounds, then bring your attention to the center of the group."

4. "Let's have the drums alternate playing with the xylophones for approximately 30 seconds each."

5. "Each of you needs to play at least three instruments; begin and end the piece with the same instrument."

Interpersonal Givens (stipulate *who* will be relating to *whom* and in what manner)

1. "Take turns improvising alone."

2. "Imitate the leader."

3. "Play in one dyad, then the other."

4. "Move around the room while playing, and make eye contact with at least two other people."

5. "Ignore the person in the group with whom you have the most conflict."

_____

Appendix F
IAP Profiles and Scales (adapted from Bruscia, 1987)

Profiles:

1. *Salience.* This profile deals with how certain musical elements are given more prominence and control than others. The five gradients are:

 Receding/Conforming/Contributing/Controlling/Overpowering

2. *Integration.* This profile deals with how simultaneous aspects of the music are organized. The five gradients are:

 Undifferentiated/Fused/Integrated/Differentiated/Overdifferentiated

3. *Variability.* This profile deals with how sequential aspects of the music are organized and related. The five gradients are:

 Rigid/Stable/Variable/Contrasting/Random

4. *Tension.* This profile deals with how much tension is created within and through various aspects of the music. The five gradients are:

 Hypotense/Calm/Cyclic/Tense/Hypertense

5. *Congruence.* This profile deals with the extent to which simultaneous feeling states and role relationships are congruent. The five gradients are:

 Uncommitted/Congruent/Centered/Incongruent/Polarized

6. *Autonomy.* This profile deals with the kinds of role relationships formed between the improvisers. The five gradients are:

 Dependent/Follower/Partner/Leader/Resister

Integration

RHY INT	Rhythmic Integration (Figure-Ground and Part-Whole)
MEL INT	Melodic Integration (Figure-Ground and Part-Whole)
HAR INT	Harmonic Integration (Figure-Ground)
TEX INT	Textural Integration (Part-Whole and Register & Configurations)
PHR INT	Phrasing Integration
TIM INT	Timbre Integration
VOL INT	Volume Integration

Variability

TEM VAR	Tempo Variability
MET VAR	Meter Variability
RHY VAR	Rhythmic Figure Variability
MEL VAR	Melodic Figure Variability
TON VAR	Tonal Ground Variability (Modality & Tonality)
HAR VAR	Harmonic Variability
TEX VAR	Texture Variability (Overall, Roles, Register, and Configurations)
STY VAR	Style Variability
PHR VAR	Phrasing Variability
TIM VAR	Timbre Variability
VOL VAR	Volume Variability

Tension

RHY TEN	Rhythmic Tension (Figure-Ground and Rhythmic Figure)
TON TEN	Tonal Tension
MEL TEN	Melodic Tension
HAR TEN	Harmonic Tension
TEX TEN	Textural Tension
PHR TEN	Phrasing Tension
VOL TEN	Volume Tension
TIM TEN	Timbral Tension

Congruence

RHY CON	Rhythmic Congruence
TON CON	Tonal Congruence
TEX CON	Textural Congruence
PHR CON	Phrasing Congruence
VOL CON	Volume Congruence
TIM CON	Timbral Congruence
BOD CON	Body Congruence
PRO CON	Program Congruence
VER CON	Verbal Congruence
INT CON	Interpersonal Congruence

Autonomy

RHY AUT	Rhythmic Autonomy (Ground and Figure)
TON AUT	Tonal Autonomy
MEL AUT	Melodic Autonomy
HAR AUT	Harmonic Autonomy
TEX AUT	Textural Autonomy
PHR AUT	Phrasing Autonomy
VOL AUT	Volume Autonomy
TIM AUT	Timbre Autonomy

REFERENCES

Aigen, K. (1998). *Paths of development in Nordoff-Robbins music therapy.* Gilsum, NH: Barcelona.

Alvin, J. (1982). Free improvisation in individual therapy. *British Journal of Music Therapy, 13*(2), 9–12.

American Music Therapy Association (1999). *Professional competencies.* Silver Spring, MD: AMTA.

Amir, D. (1996). Experiencing music therapy: Meaningful moments in the music therapy process. In M. Langenberg, K. Aigen, & J. Frommer (Eds*.), Qualitative music therapy research: Beginning dialogues* (pp. 109–129). Gilsum: NH: Barcelona.

Austin, D. (1998). When the psyche sings: Transference and countertransference in improvised singing with individual adults. In K. Bruscia (Ed*.), The dynamics of music psychotherapy* (pp. 315–333). Gilsum, NH: Barcelona.

Borczon, R. (2004). *Music therapy: A fieldwork primer.* Gilsum, NH: Barcelona.

Boxill, E. (1985). *Music therapy for the developmentally disabled.* Austin, TX: Pro-Ed.

Boyd, B. (1992). *Exploring jazz scales for keyboard.* Milwaukee, WI: Hal Leonard.

Bruscia, K. (1987*). Improvisational models of music therapy.* Springfield, IL: Charles C. Thomas.

Bruscia, K. (1989). The practical side of improvisational music therapy. *Music Therapy Perspectives, 6,* 11–15.

Bruscia, K. (1998). *Defining music therapy* (2nd ed.). Gilsum, NH: Barcelona.

Bruscia, K. (2001). A qualitative approach to analyzing client improvisations. *Music Therapy Perspectives, 19*(1), 7–21.

Certification Board for Music Therapists (2004). *Scope of practice.* Downington, PA: CBMT.

Corey, G., Corey, M., Callanan, P., & Russell, J. (2004). *Group techniques* (3rd ed.). Pacific Grove, CA: Brooks/Cole.

Darnley-Smith, R., & Patey, H. (2003). *Music therapy.* London: Sage.

Forinash, M., & Gonzalez, D. (1989). A phenomenological perspective of music therapy. *Music Therapy, 8,* 35–46.

Gardstrom, S. (2001). Practical techniques for the development of complementary skills in clinical improvisation. *Music Therapy Perspectives, 19*(2), 82–87.

Gardstrom, S. (2004). An investigation of meaning in clinical music improvisation with troubled adolescents. In B. Abrams (Ed.), *Qualitative inquiries in music therapy: A monograph series* (pp. 77–160). Gilsum, NH: Barcelona.

Hadsell, N. (1993). Levels of external structure in music therapy. *Music Therapy Perspectives, 11*(2), 61–65.

Henderson, H. (1991). Improvised song stories in the treatment of a 13-year-old sexually abused girl from the Xhosa tribe in South Africa. In K. Bruscia (Ed.), *Case studies in music therapy* (pp. 207–217). Phoenixville, PA: Barcelona.

Hiller, J. (2006). Use of and training in clinical improvisation among music therapists educated in the United States. Unpublished survey.

Hull, A. (2006). What is a community drum circle? Retrieved December 25, 2006, from http://drumcircle.com/arthurian/communitydc.html.

Kowski, J. (2003). Growing up alone: Analytical music therapy with children of parents treated with a drug and substance abuse program. In S. Hadley (Ed.), *Psychodynamic music therapy: Case* studies (pp. 87–104). Gilsum, NH: Barcelona.

Loth, H. (2002). "There's no getting away from anything in here": A music therapy group within an inpatient programme for adults with eating disorders. In A.Davies and M. Jenkyns (Eds.), *Music therapy and group work* (pp. 90–104). London: Jessica Kingsley.

McGuire, M., & Smeltekop, R. (1994) Termination in music therapy I: Theory and clinical applications. *Music Therapy Perspectives, 12*(1), 20–27.

McGuire, M., & Smeltekop, R. (1994) Termination in music therapy II: A model and clinical applications. *Music Therapy Perspectives, 12*(1), 28–34.

Miller, H. (1991). Group improvisation therapy: The experience of one man with schizophrenia. In K. Bruscia (Ed.), *Case studies in music therapy* (pp. 417–431). Phoenixville, PA: Barcelona.

Meier, S., & Davis, S. (2001). *The elements of counseling* (4th ed.). Belmont, CA: Brooks/Cole-Thomson.

Meyer, L. (1956). *Emotion and meaning in music.* Chicago: University of Chicago Press.

Montello, L. (1998). Relational issues in psychoanalytic music therapy with traumatized individuals. In K. Bruscia (Ed.), *The dynamics of music psychotherapy* (pp. 299–313).Gilsum, NH: Barcelona.

Montello, L. (2003). Protect this child: Psychodynamic music therapy with a gifted child. In S. Hadley (Ed.), *Psychodynamic music therapy: Case* studies (pp. 299–318). Gilsum, NH: Barcelona.

Murow, E. (2002). Working as a music therapist in Mexico. *Voices: A World Forum for Music Therapy*. Retrieved December 25, 2006, from http://www.voices.no/mainissues/Voices2(2)murow.html.

Jewell, E., & Abate, F. (Eds.). (2001). *The new Oxford American dictionary* New York: Oxford Press.

Nolan, P. (2003). Through music to therapeutic attachment: Psychodynamic music psychotherapy with a musician with dysthmymic disorder. In S. Hadley (Ed.), *Psychodynamic music therapy: Case studies* (pp. 319–338).Gilsum, NH: Barcelona.

Nordoff, P., and Robbins, C. (1977*). Creative music therapy: Individualized treatment for the handicapped child.* New York: John Day.

Okun, B. (2001). Effective helping: Interviewing and counseling techniques (6th ed.). Belmont, CA: Thomson Book/Cole Publishing.

Pavlicevic, M. (1997). *Music therapy in context: music, meaning and relationship.* London: Jessica Kingsley.

Priestley, M. (1975). *Music therapy in action.* London: Constable.

Priestley, M. (1994). *Essays on Analytical Music Therapy*. Gilsum, NH: Barcelona.

Robarts, J. (2003). The healing function of improvised songs in music therapy with a child survivor of early trauma and sexual abuse. In S. Hadley (Ed.), *Psychodynamic music therapy: Case studies* (pp. 141–182). Gilsum, NH: Barcelona.

Robbins, C., & Robbins, C. (1998). *Healing heritage: Paul Nordoff exploring the tonal language of music.* Gilsum, NH: Barcelona.

Smeijsters, H. (2005). *Sounding the self: Analogy in improvisational music therapy.* Gilsum, NH: Barcelona.

Stephens, G. (1984). Group supervision in music therapy. *Music Therapy, 4*(1), 29–38.

Stephens, G. (1985). Answers to a Questionnaire by Kenneth Bruscia. Unpublished data. In K. Bruscia, *Improvisational models of music therapy* (p. 338). Springfield, IL: Charles C. Thomas.

Towse, E. & Roberts,C. (2002). Supervising a music therapy group: A seriously non-musical problem. In A. Davies and M. Jenkyns (Eds.), *Music therapy and group work* (pp. 249–261). London: Jessica Kingsley.

Wheeler, B. (2003). A psychotherapeutic classification of music therapy practices: A continuum of procedures. *Music Therapy Perspectives, 1,* 8–16.

Wigram, T. (2004). *Improvisation: Methods and techniques for music therapy clinicians, educators, and students.* London: Jessica Kingsley.

Yalom, I. (1975). *The theory and practice of group psychotherapy.* New York: Basic Books.

AUTHOR INDEX

Aigen, K., 71
Alvin, J., 17
Amir, D., 110
Austin, D., 115
Borczon, R., 143
Boxill, E., 112
Boyd, B., 59
Bruscia, K., 1, 8, 14–17, 19, 20, 45, 52, 95–104, 106, 108, 110–116, 120, 122, 123, 126, 127, 129–131, 133, 134, 137, 140
Callanan, P., 140
Corey, G., 140
Corey, M., 140
Darnley-Smith, R., 6, 96, 100, 105, 106
Davies, A., 43, 47
Davis, S., 140
Dvorkin, J., 77
Forinash, M., 100
Gardstrom, S., 17, 35, 142
Gonzalez, D., 100
Hadsell, N., 69
Henderson, H., 91
Hiller, J., 2, 7, 12, 13
Hull, A., 21
Jenkyns, M., 43, 47
Kowski, J., 115
Loth, H., 47
McGuire, M., 138
Meier, S., 140
Meyer, L., 16
Miller, H., 104
Montello, L., 108, 116
Murow, E., 46
Nolan, P., 97, 109
Nordoff, P., 14, 71
Okun, B., 140, 141, 146
Patey, H., 6, 96, 105, 106